GRAPHIC LIBRARY™

D1217054

GRAPHIC HISTORY

DOLLEY MADISON
SAVES HISTORY

by Roger Smalley

illustrated by Anna Maria Cool,
Scott Rosema, and Charles Barnett III

Consultant: Kenneth Madison Clark, Historical Consultant,

The James Madison Museum

Orange, Virginia

Capstone press

Mankato, Minnesota

Graphic Library is published by Capstone Press,
151 Good Counsel Drive, P.O. Box 669, Mankato, Minnesota 56002.
www.capstonepub.com

Printed in the United States of America in Stevens Point, Wisconsion.

082011
006341R

Books published by Capstone Press are manufactured with paper containing at least 10 percent post-consumer waste.

Library of Congress Cataloging-in-Publication Data
Smalley, Roger.
Dolley Madison saves history / by Roger Smalley; illustrated by Anna Maria Cool, Scott Rosema, Charles Barnett III.
p. cm. —(Graphic library. Graphic history)
Includes bibliographical references and index.
ISBN-13: 978-0-7368-4972-2 (hardcover)
ISBN-10: 0-7368-4972-6 (hardcover)
ISBN-13: 978-0-7368-6205-9 (softcover)
ISBN-10: 0-7368-6205-6 (softcover)
1. Madison, Dolley, 1768–1849—Juvenile literature. 2. Presidents' spouses—United States—Biography—Juvenile literature. 3. United States—History—War of 1812—Juvenile literature. 4. Washington (D.C.)—History—Capture by the British, 1814—Juvenile literature. I. Cool, Anna Maria. II. Rosema, Scott. III. Barnett, Charles, III. IV. Title. V. Series.
E342.1.S63 2006
973.5'1'092—dc22 2005008465

Summary: The story of Dolley Madison's actions during the War of 1812 is told in a graphic novel format.

Art and Editorial Direction
Jason Knudson and Blake A. Hoena

Designers
Bob Lentz and Juliette Peters

Colorist
Sarah Trover

Editor
Sarah L. Schuette

Editor's note: Direct quotations from primary sources are indicated by a yellow background.

Direct quotations appear on the following pages:
Pages 4, 8, 11, 17, 19, 25 from *The Selected Letters of Dolley Payne Madison* by Dolley Madison (Charlottesville, VA: University of Virginia Press, 2003.).
Pages 6, 9, 13 from *The First Forty Years of Washington Society in the Family Letters of Margaret Bayard Smith* by Margaret Bayard Smith (New York: F. Ungar, 1965).
Pages 21, 23 from *The Burning of Washington: The British Invasion of 1814* by Anthony S. Pitch (Annapolis, MD: Naval Institute Press, 1998).

TABLE OF CONTENTS

CHAPTER 1

THE MADISONS GO TO WASHINGTON

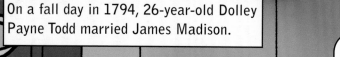

On a fall day in 1794, 26-year-old Dolley Payne Todd married James Madison.

Congratulations!

Today, I have married the man I most admire.

Years earlier, James helped write the United States Constitution and was very involved in the politics of the newly formed nation.

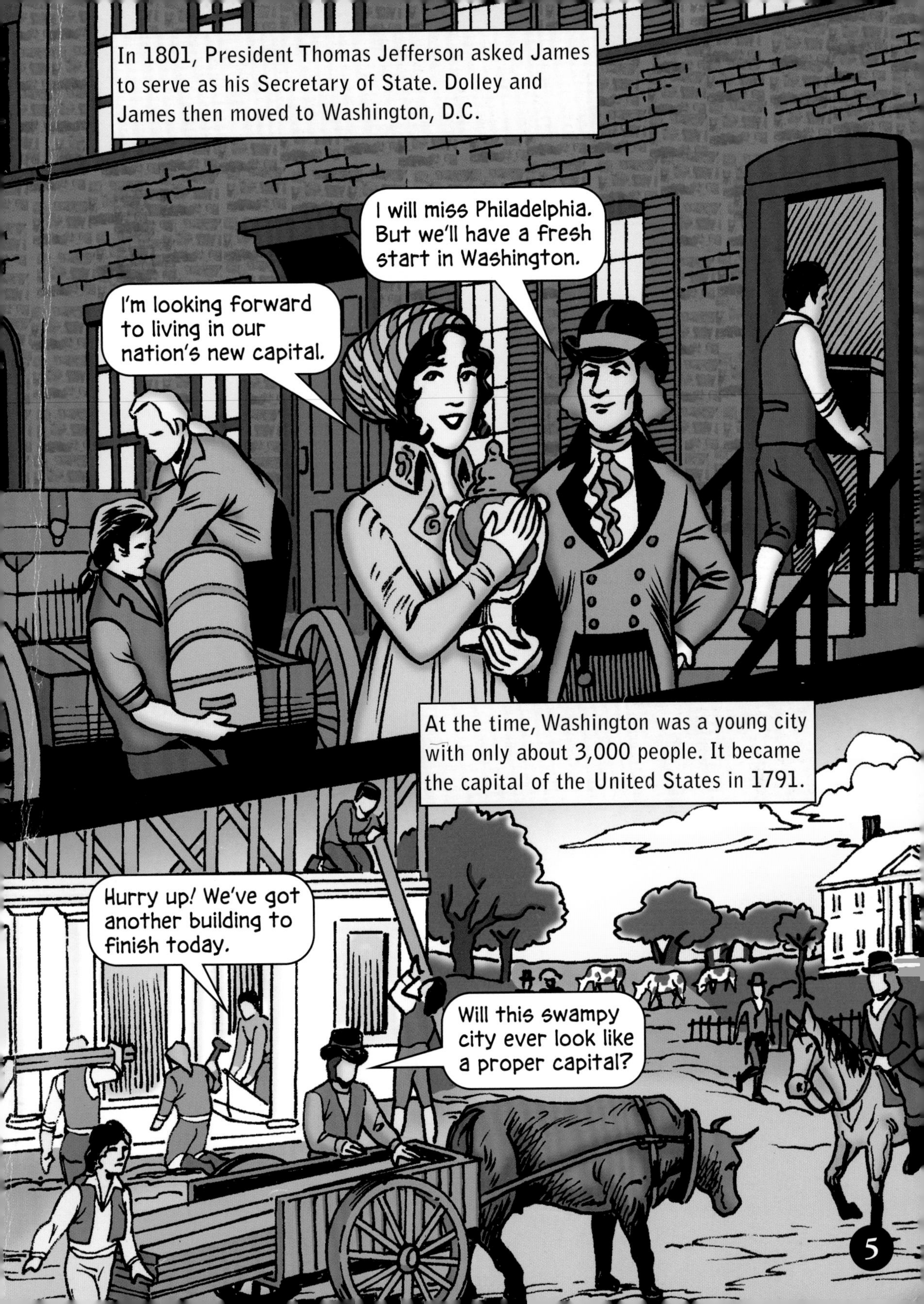
In 1801, President Thomas Jefferson asked James to serve as his Secretary of State. Dolley and James then moved to Washington, D.C.
I'm looking forward to living in our nation's new capital.
I will miss Philadelphia. But we'll have a fresh start in Washington.
At the time, Washington was a young city with only about 3,000 people. It became the capital of the United States in 1791.
Hurry up! We've got another building to finish today.
Will this swampy city ever look like a proper capital?

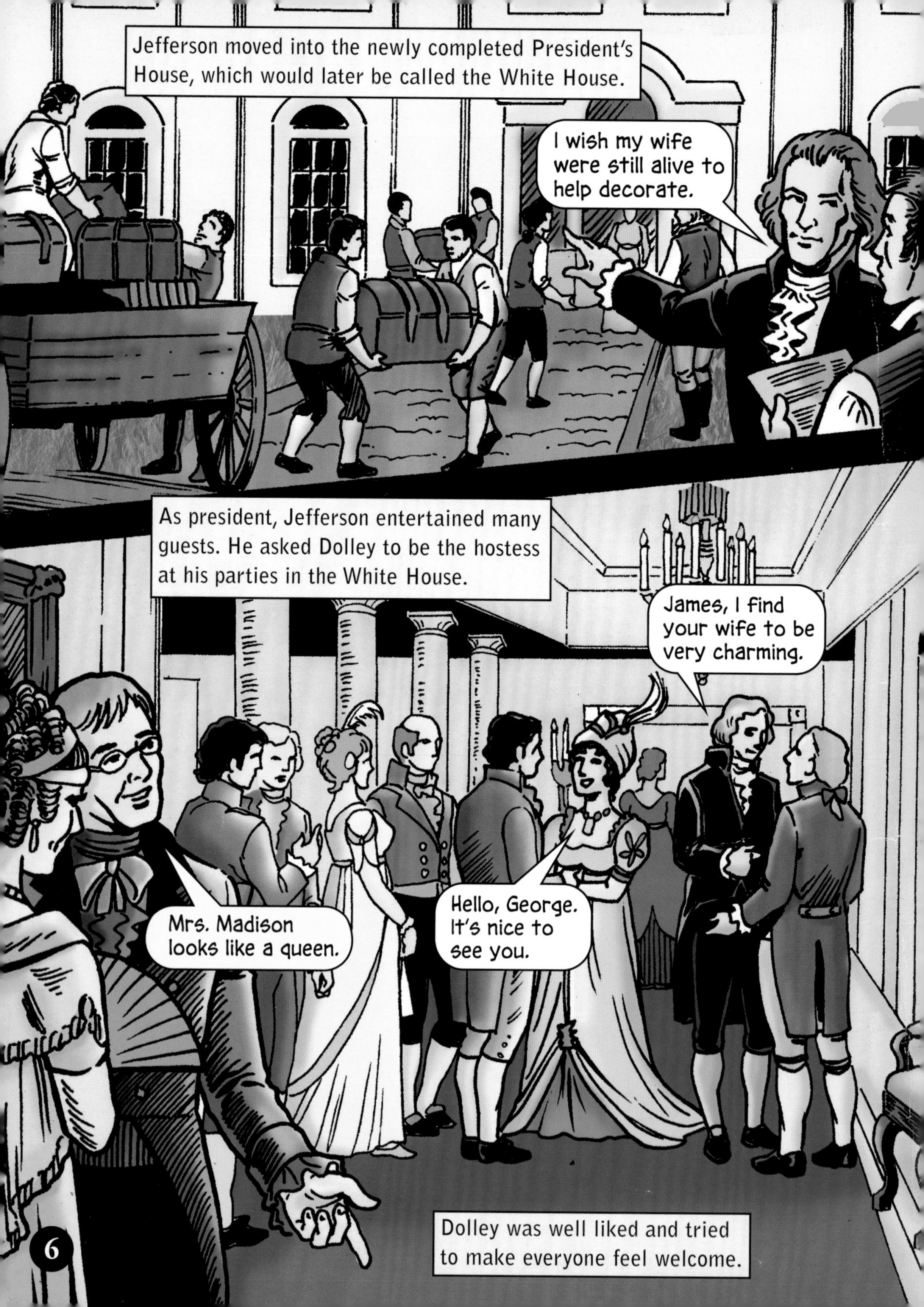
Jefferson moved into the newly completed President's House, which would later be called the White House.
I wish my wife were still alive to help decorate.
As president, Jefferson entertained many guests. He asked Dolley to be the hostess at his parties in the White House.
James, I find your wife to be very charming.
Hello, George. It's nice to see you.
Mrs. Madison looks like a queen.
Dolley was well liked and tried to make everyone feel welcome.

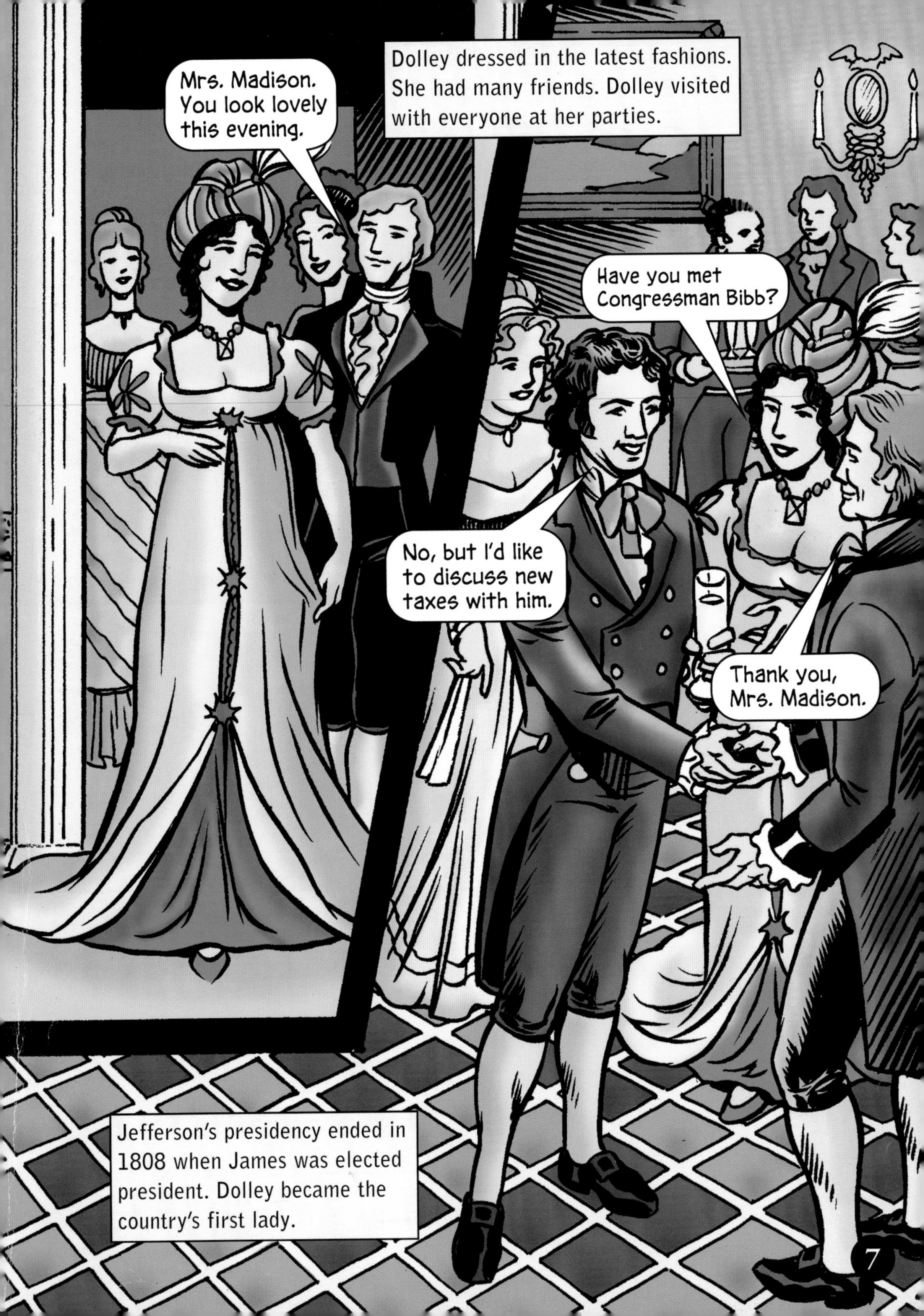
Mrs. Madison. You look lovely this evening.
Dolley dressed in the latest fashions. She had many friends. Dolley visited with everyone at her parties.
Have you met Congressman Bibb?
No, but I'd like to discuss new taxes with him.
Thank you, Mrs. Madison.
Jefferson's presidency ended in 1808 when James was elected president. Dolley became the country's first lady.

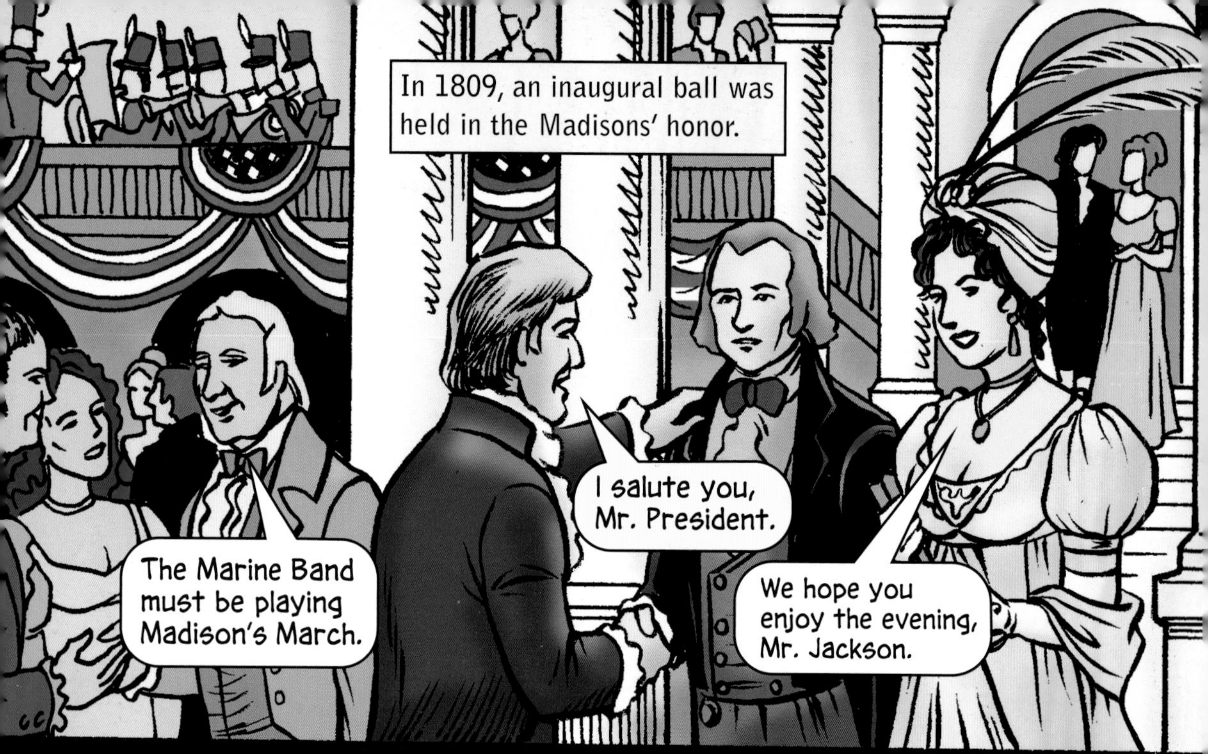
In 1809, an inaugural ball was held in the Madisons' honor.
The Marine Band must be playing Madison's March.
I salute you, Mr. President.
We hope you enjoy the evening, Mr. Jackson.

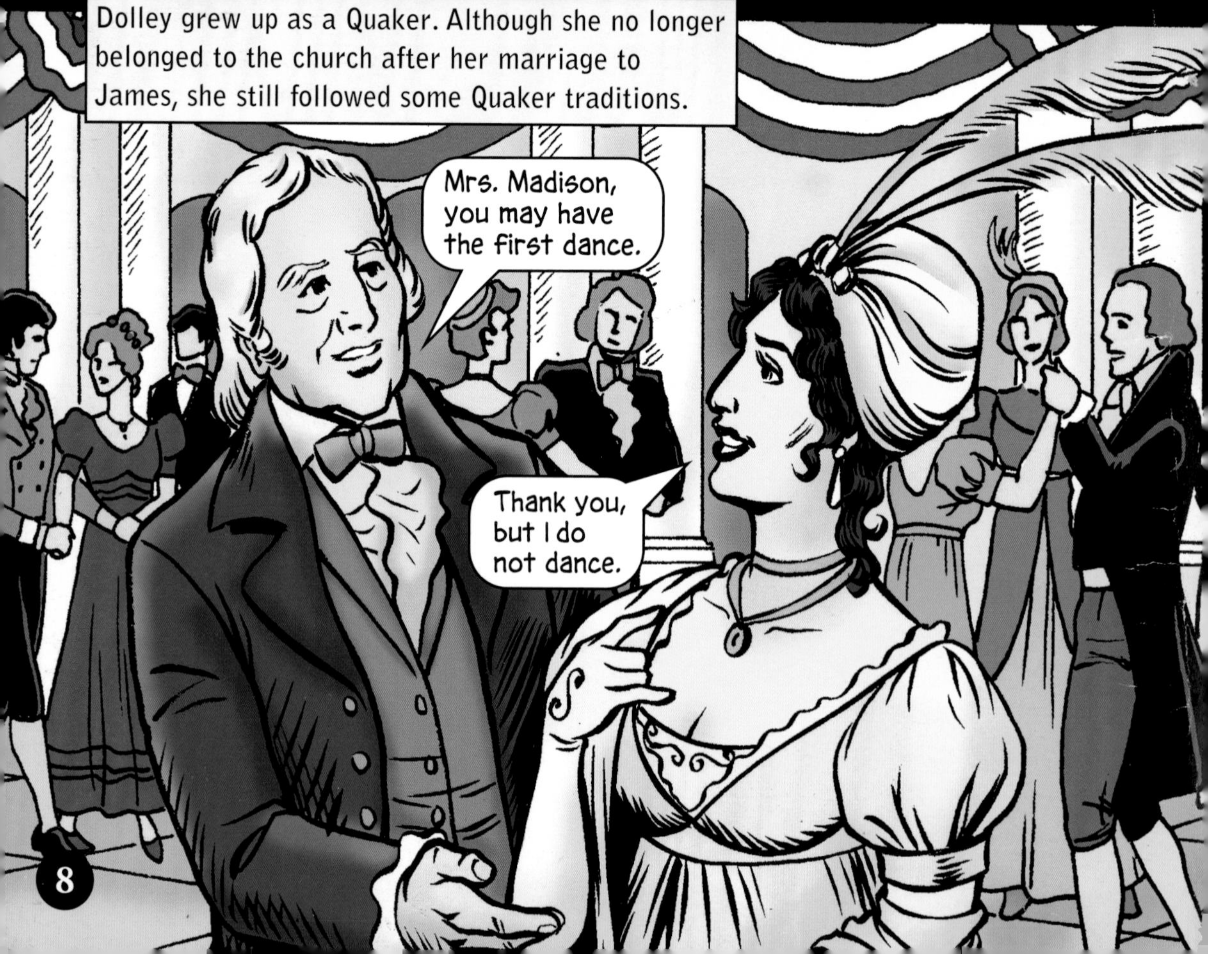
Dolley grew up as a Quaker. Although she no longer belonged to the church after her marriage to James, she still followed some Quaker traditions.
Mrs. Madison, you may have the first dance.
Thank you, but I do not dance.

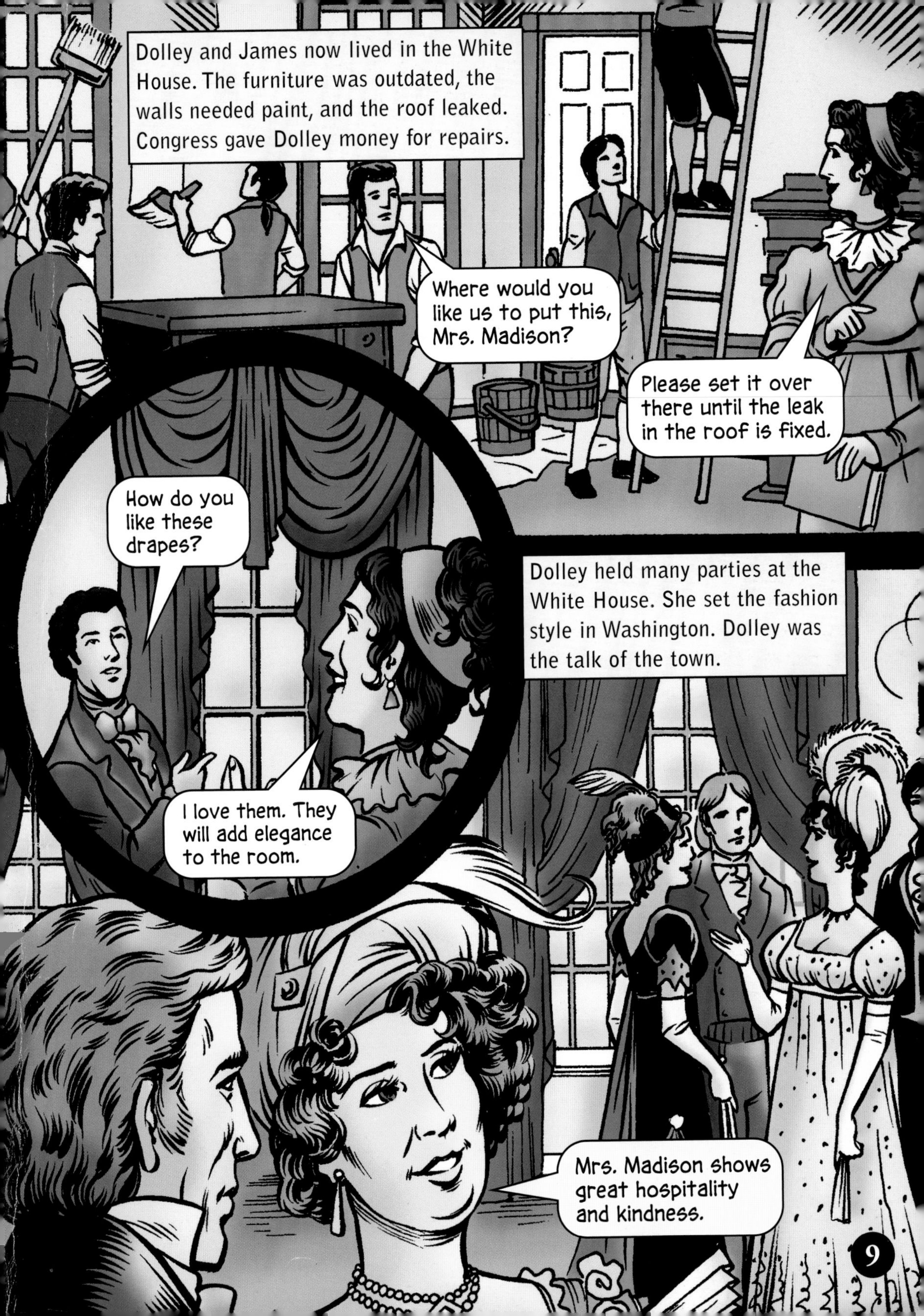

Dolley and James now lived in the White House. The furniture was outdated, the walls needed paint, and the roof leaked. Congress gave Dolley money for repairs.
Where would you like us to put this, Mrs. Madison?
Please set it over there until the leak in the roof is fixed.
How do you like these drapes?
I love them. They will add elegance to the room.
Dolley held many parties at the White House. She set the fashion style in Washington. Dolley was the talk of the town.
Mrs. Madison shows great hospitality and kindness.

Chapter 2

The War of 1812

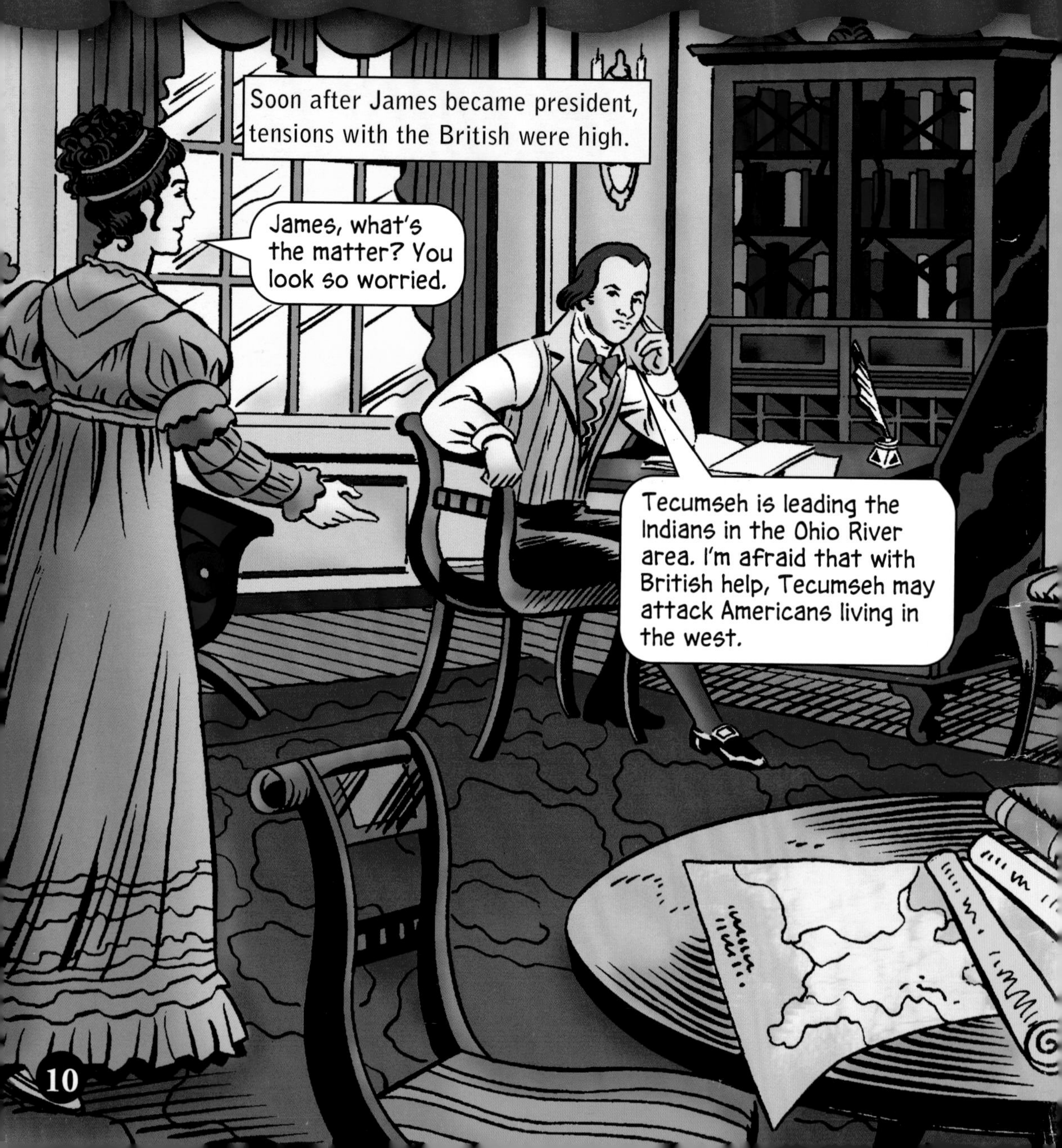

Soon after James became president, tensions with the British were high.
James, what's the matter? You look so worried.
Tecumseh is leading the Indians in the Ohio River area. I'm afraid that with British help, Tecumseh may attack Americans living in the west.

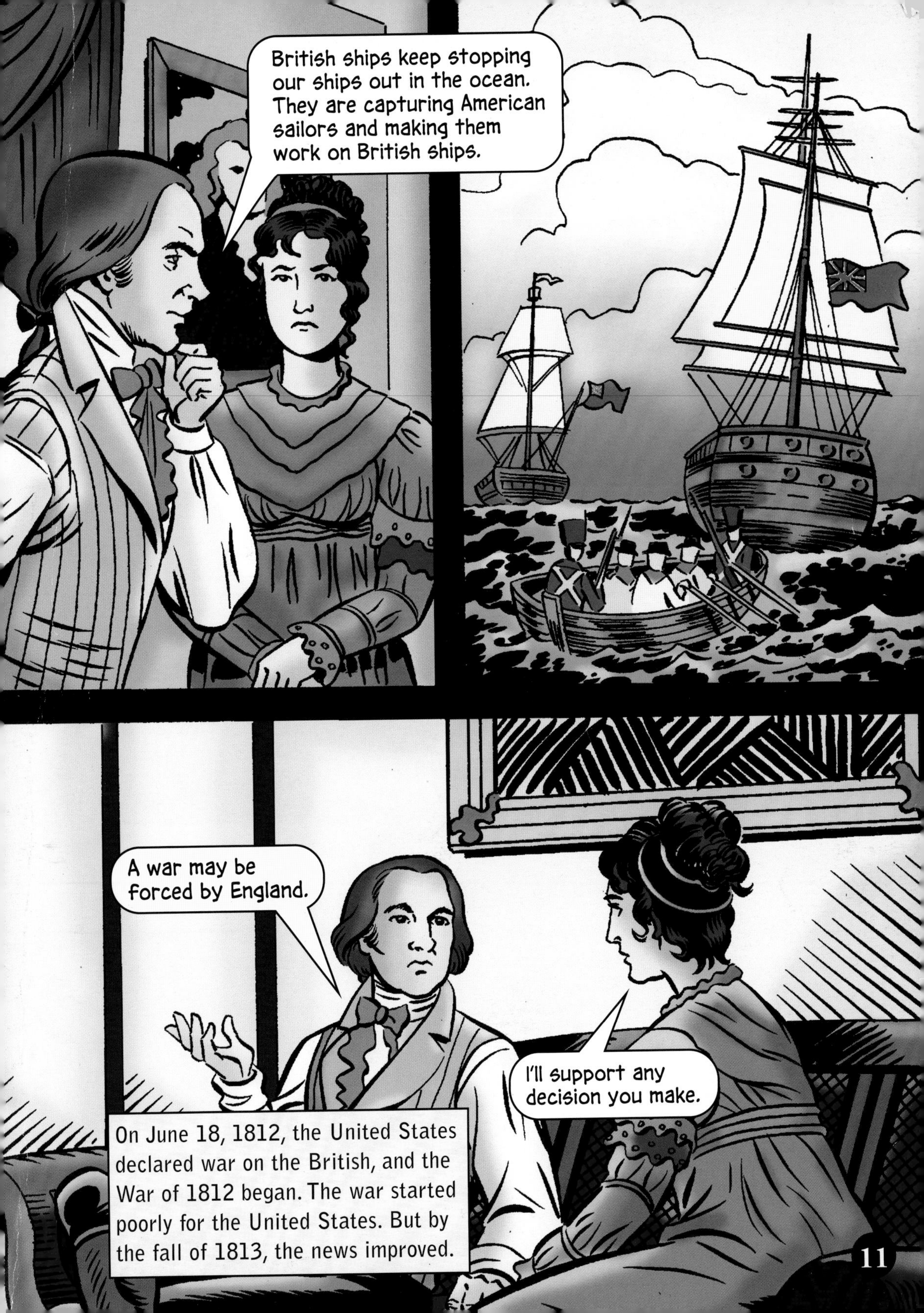
British ships keep stopping our ships out in the ocean. They are capturing American sailors and making them work on British ships.
A war may be forced by England.
I'll support any decision you make.
On June 18, 1812, the United States declared war on the British, and the War of 1812 began. The war started poorly for the United States. But by the fall of 1813, the news improved.

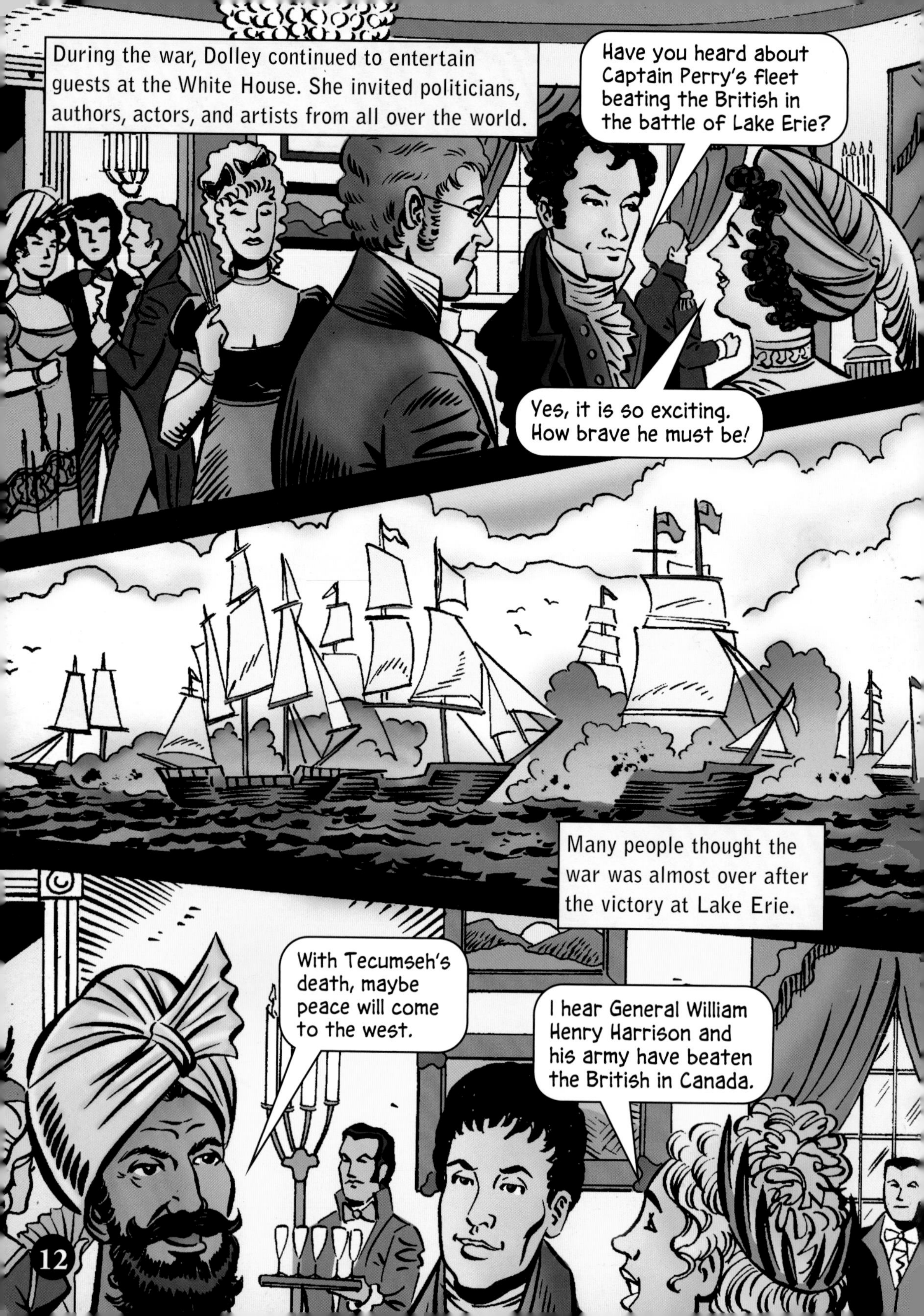
During the war, Dolley continued to entertain guests at the White House. She invited politicians, authors, actors, and artists from all over the world.
Have you heard about Captain Perry's fleet beating the British in the battle of Lake Erie?
Yes, it is so exciting. How brave he must be!
Many people thought the war was almost over after the victory at Lake Erie.
With Tecumseh's death, maybe peace will come to the west.
I hear General William Henry Harrison and his army have beaten the British in Canada.

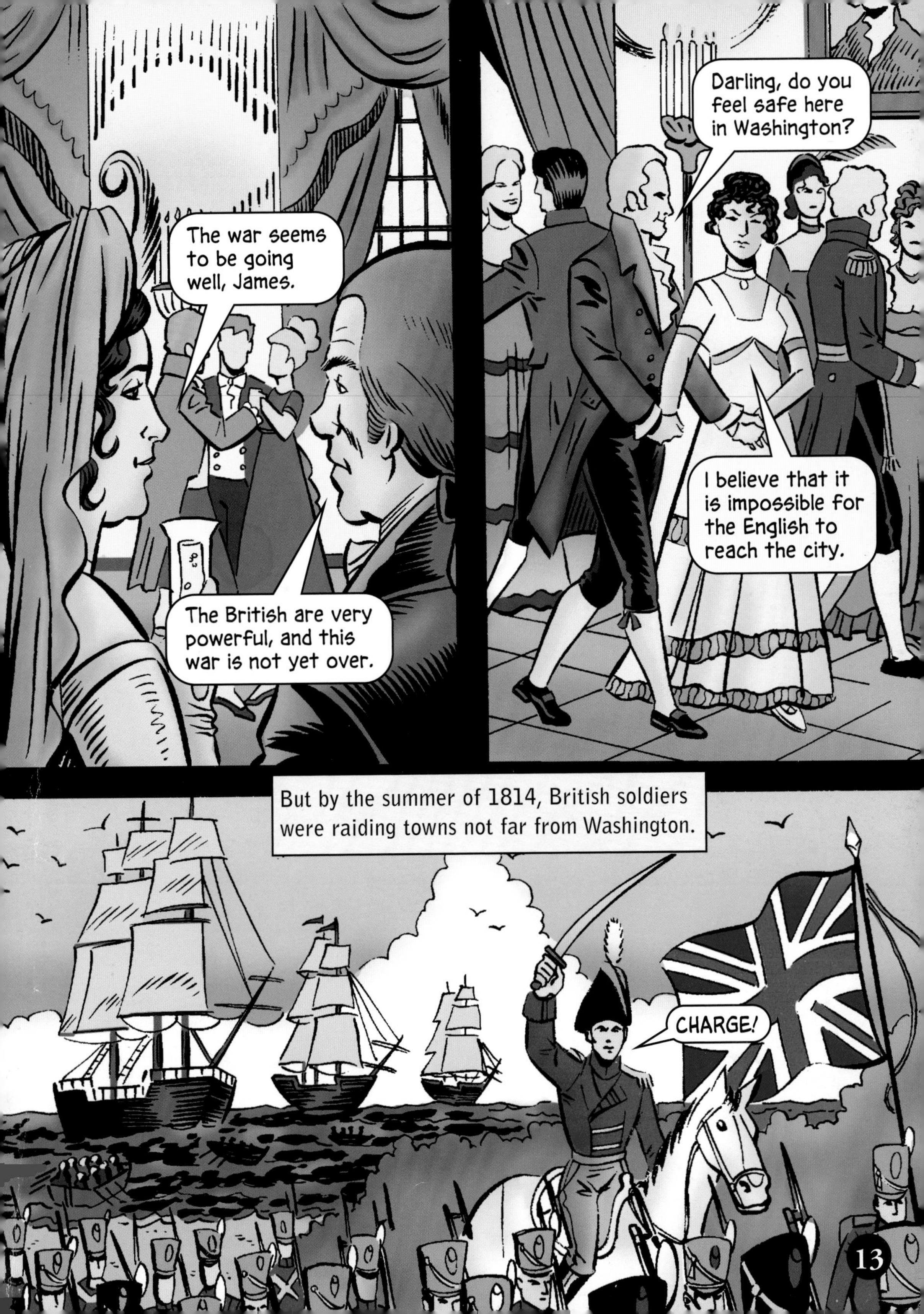
The war seems to be going well, James.
The British are very powerful, and this war is not yet over.
Darling, do you feel safe here in Washington?
I believe that it is impossible for the English to reach the city.
But by the summer of 1814, British soldiers were raiding towns not far from Washington.
CHARGE!

Chapter 3

Danger in Washington, D.C.

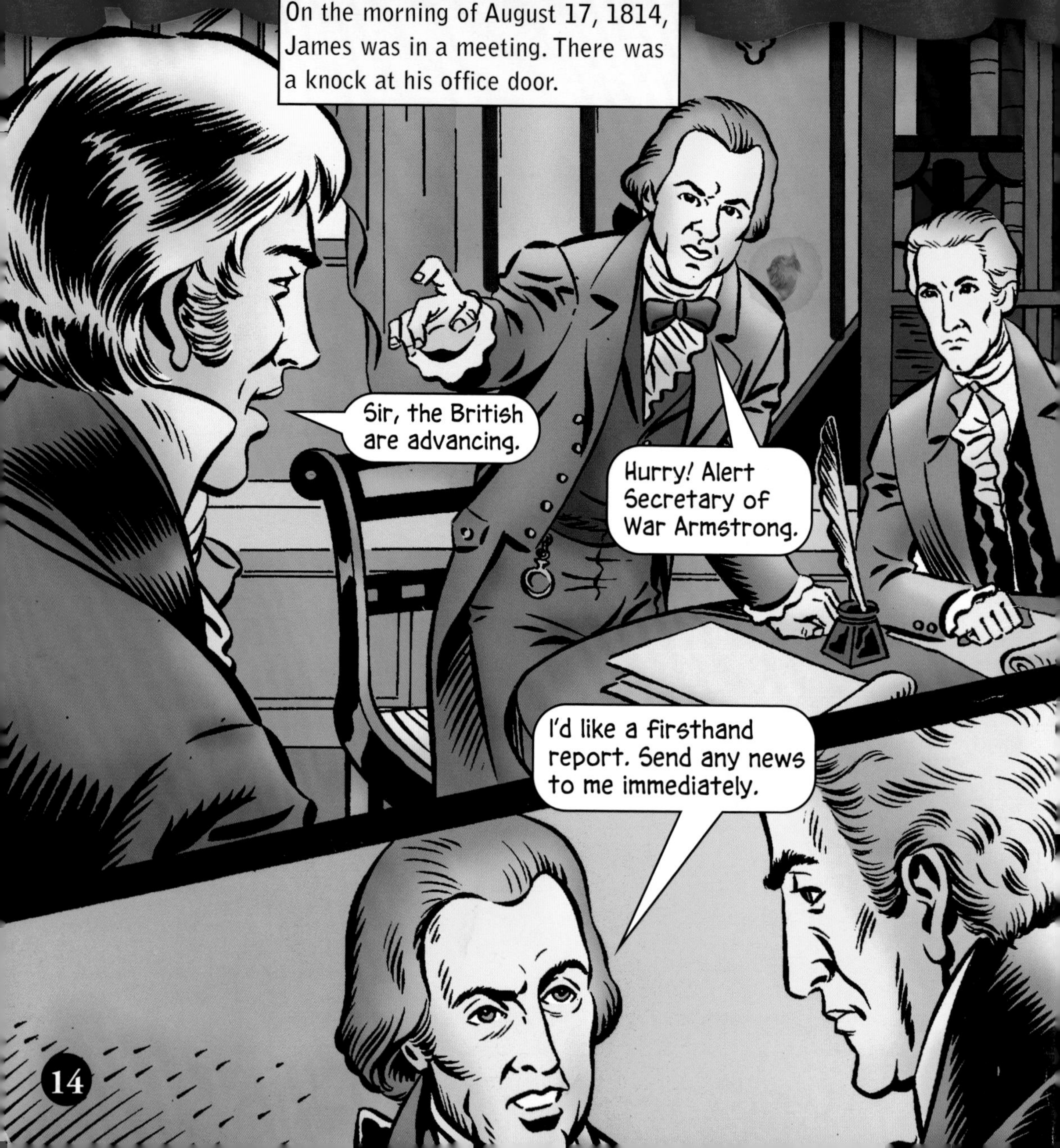
On the morning of August 17, 1814, James was in a meeting. There was a knock at his office door.
Sir, the British are advancing.
Hurry! Alert Secretary of War Armstrong.
I'd like a firsthand report. Send any news to me immediately.

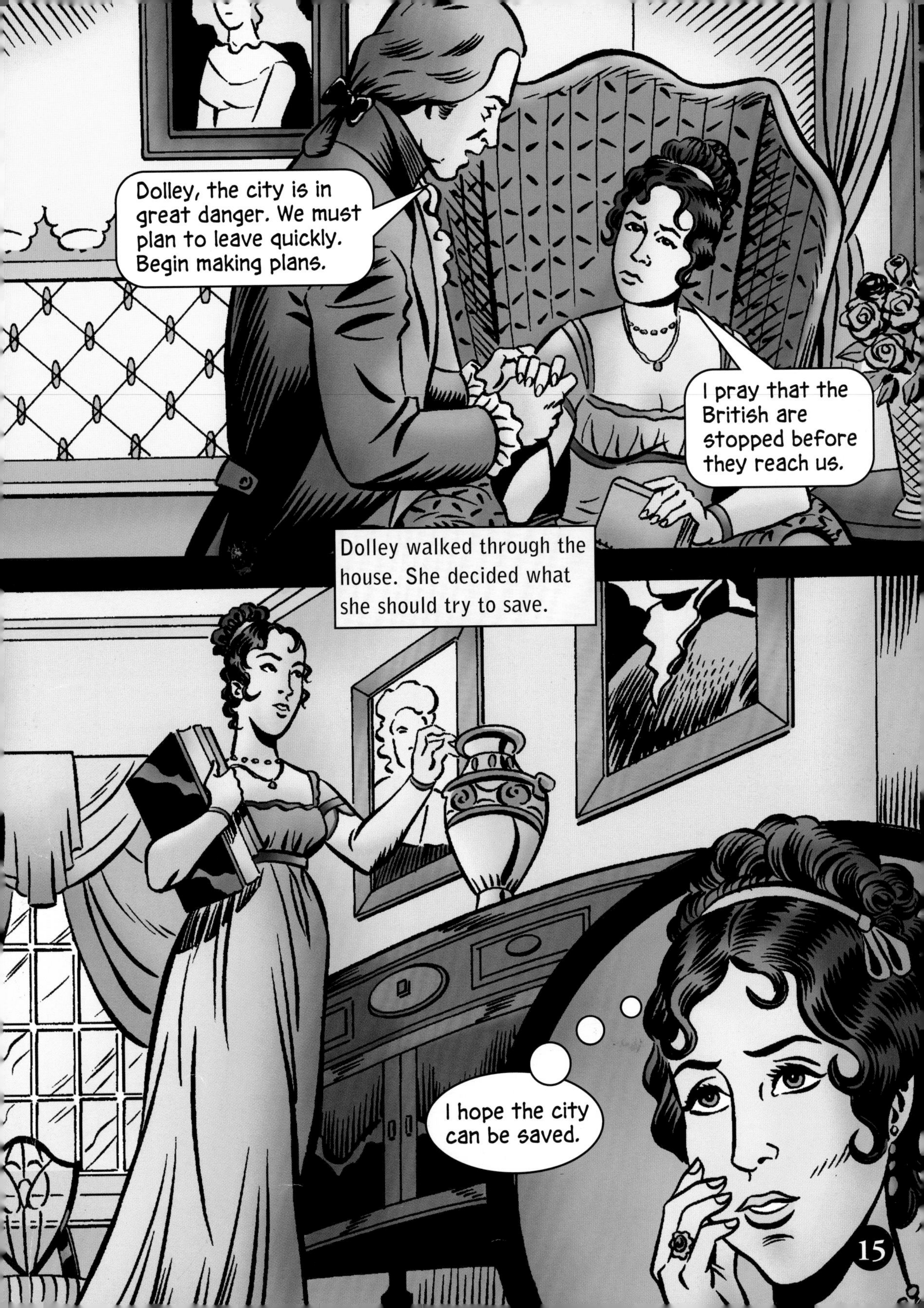
Dolley, the city is in great danger. We must plan to leave quickly. Begin making plans.
I pray that the British are stopped before they reach us.
Dolley walked through the house. She decided what she should try to save.
I hope the city can be saved.

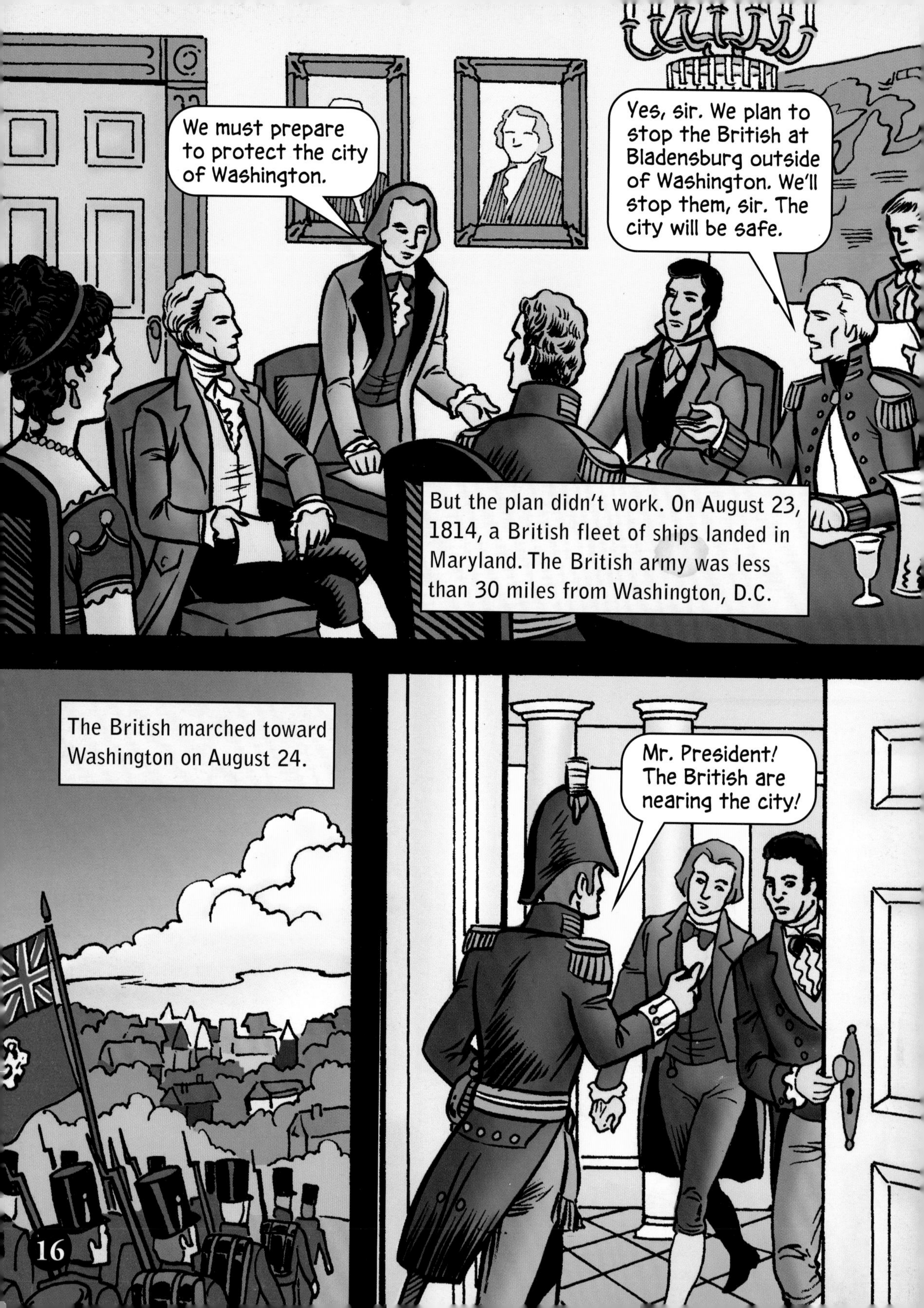
We must prepare to protect the city of Washington.
Yes, sir. We plan to stop the British at Bladensburg outside of Washington. We'll stop them, sir. The city will be safe.
But the plan didn't work. On August 23, 1814, a British fleet of ships landed in Maryland. The British army was less than 30 miles from Washington, D.C.
The British marched toward Washington on August 24.
Mr. President! The British are nearing the city!

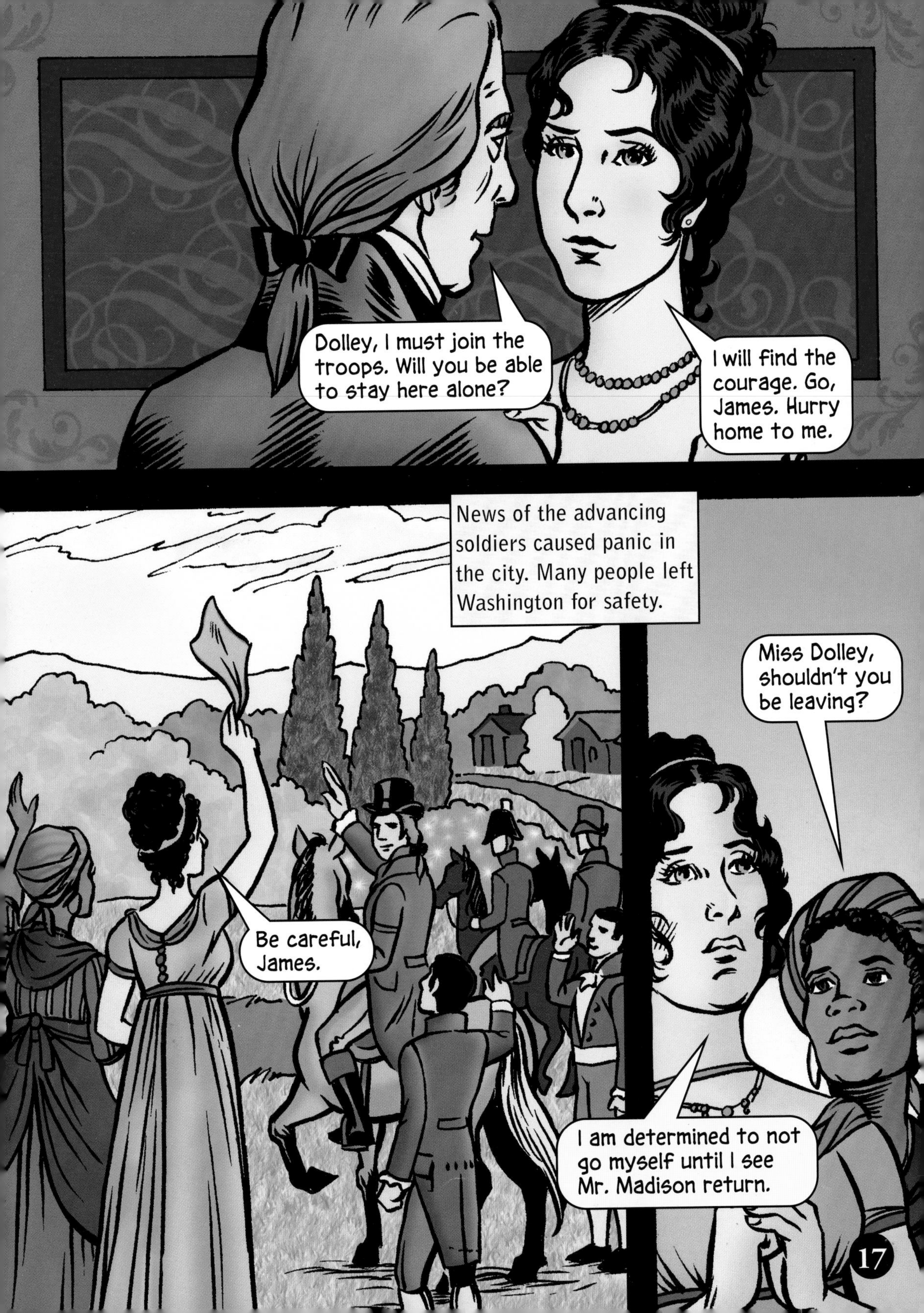

Dolley, I must join the troops. Will you be able to stay here alone?
I will find the courage. Go, James. Hurry home to me.
News of the advancing soldiers caused panic in the city. Many people left Washington for safety.
Be careful, James.
Miss Dolley, shouldn't you be leaving?
I am determined to not go myself until I see Mr. Madison return.

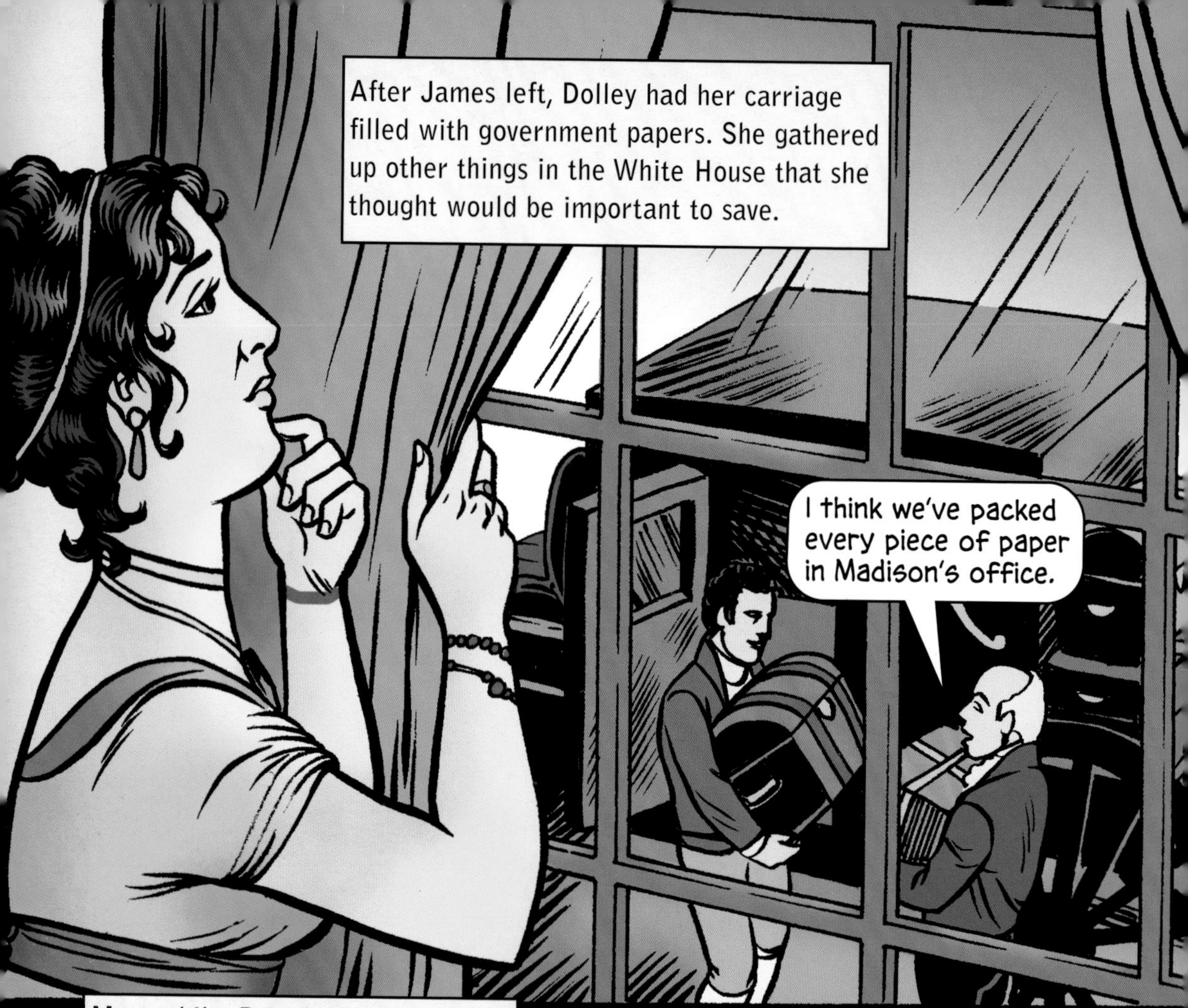
After James left, Dolley had her carriage filled with government papers. She gathered up other things in the White House that she thought would be important to save.
I think we've packed every piece of paper in Madison's office.

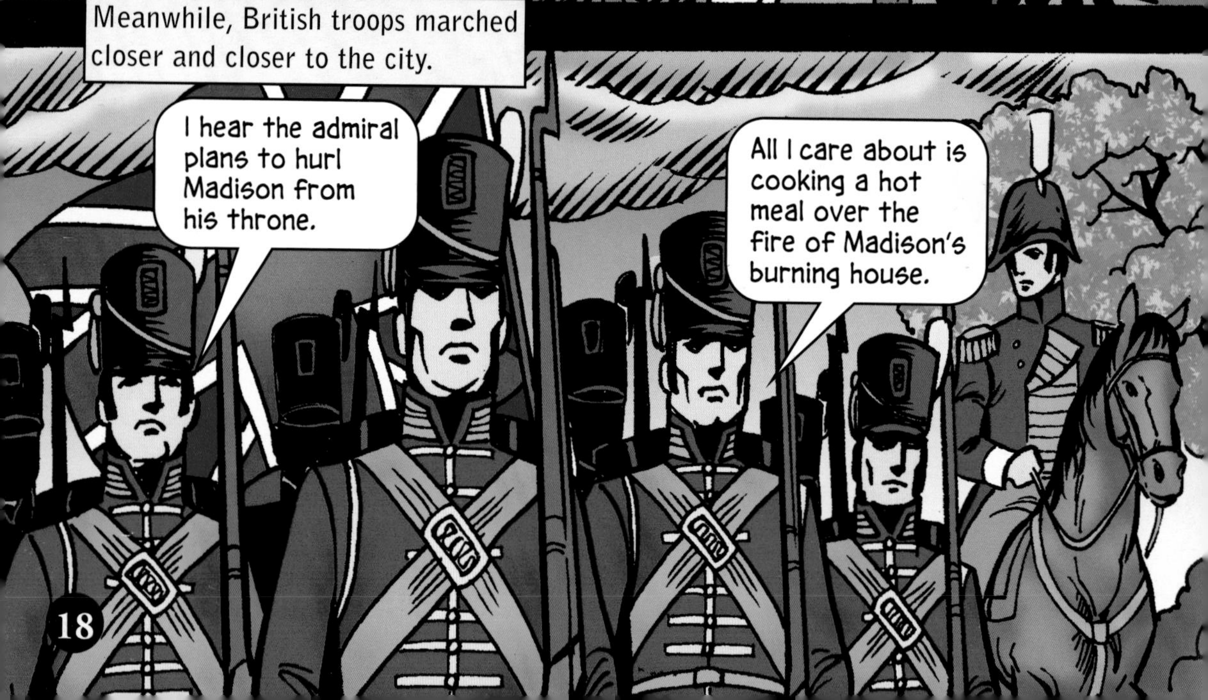
Meanwhile, British troops marched closer and closer to the city.
I hear the admiral plans to hurl Madison from his throne.
All I care about is cooking a hot meal over the fire of Madison's burning house.

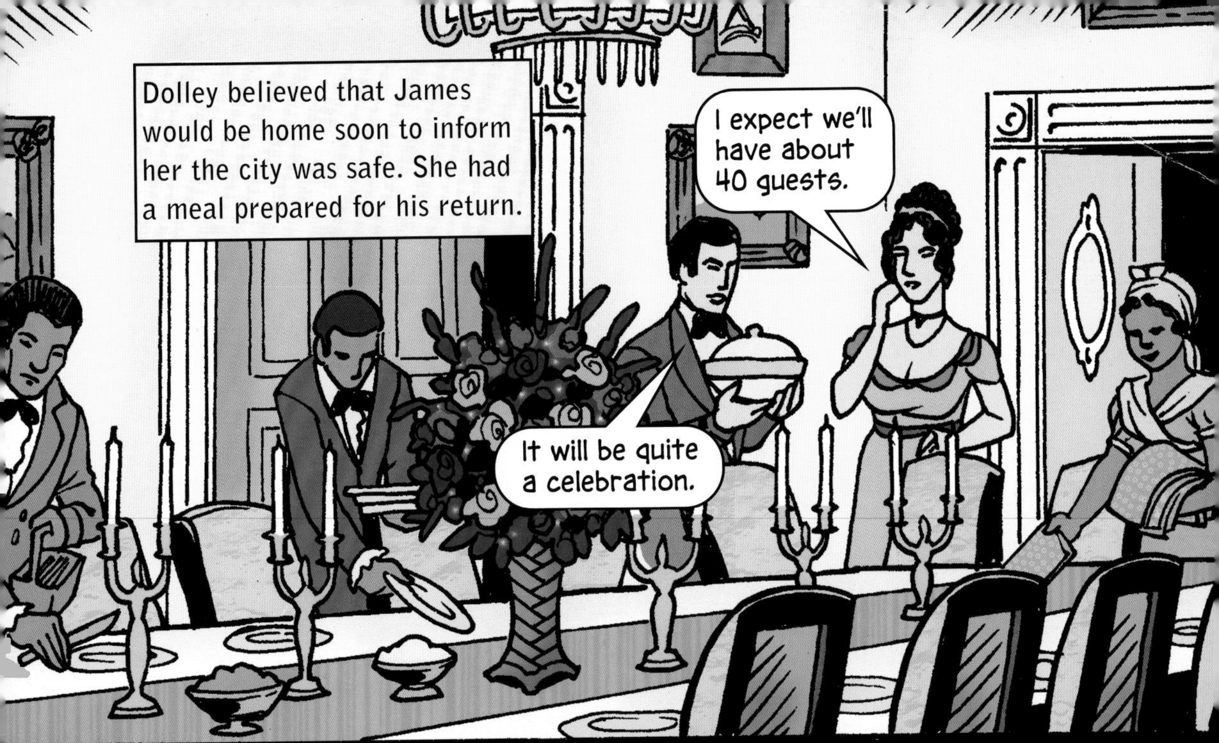
Dolley believed that James would be home soon to inform her the city was safe. She had a meal prepared for his return.
I expect we'll have about 40 guests.
It will be quite a celebration.

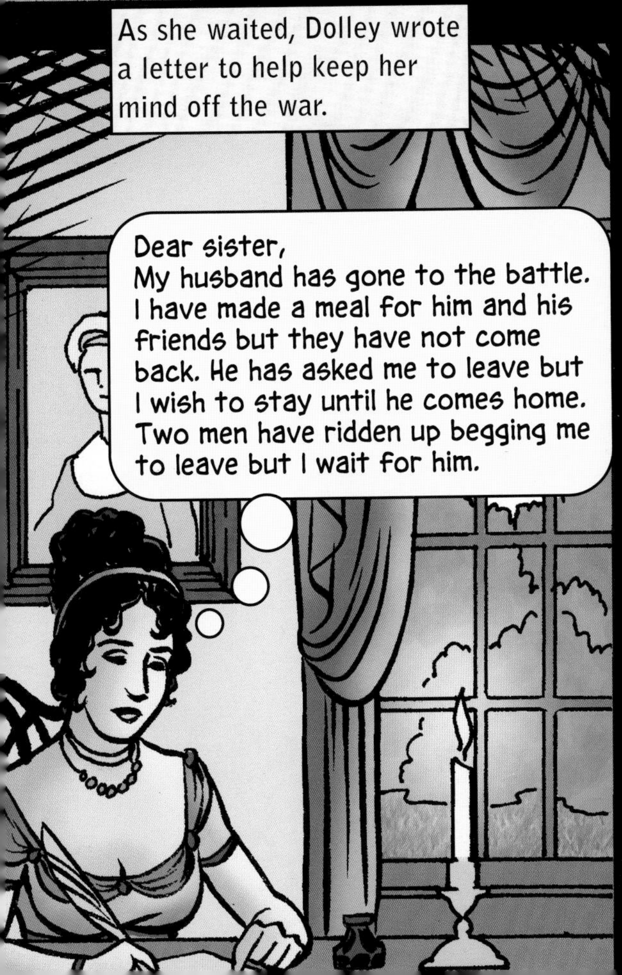
As she waited, Dolley wrote a letter to help keep her mind off the war.
Dear sister, My husband has gone to the battle. I have made a meal for him and his friends but they have not come back. He has asked me to leave but I wish to stay until he comes home. Two men have ridden up begging me to leave but I wait for him.

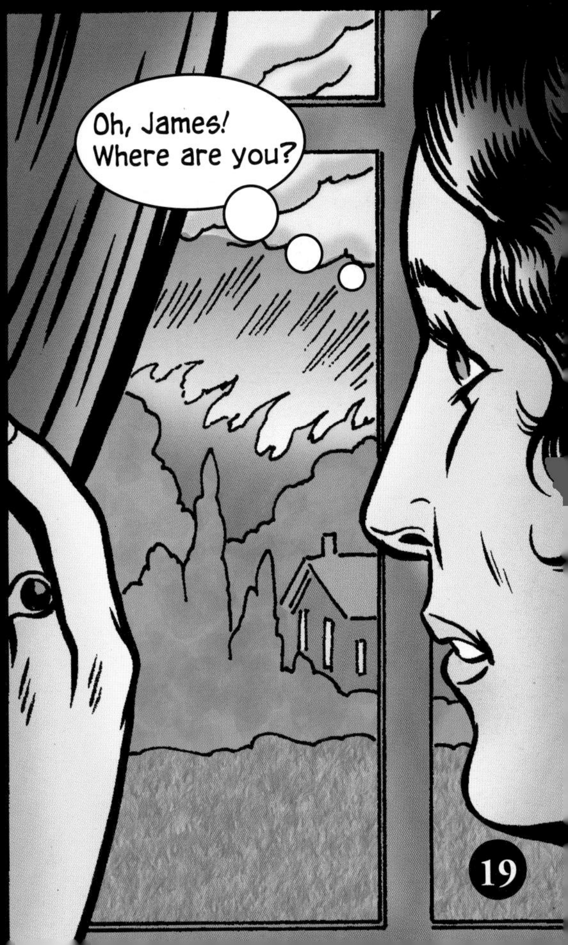
Oh, James! Where are you?

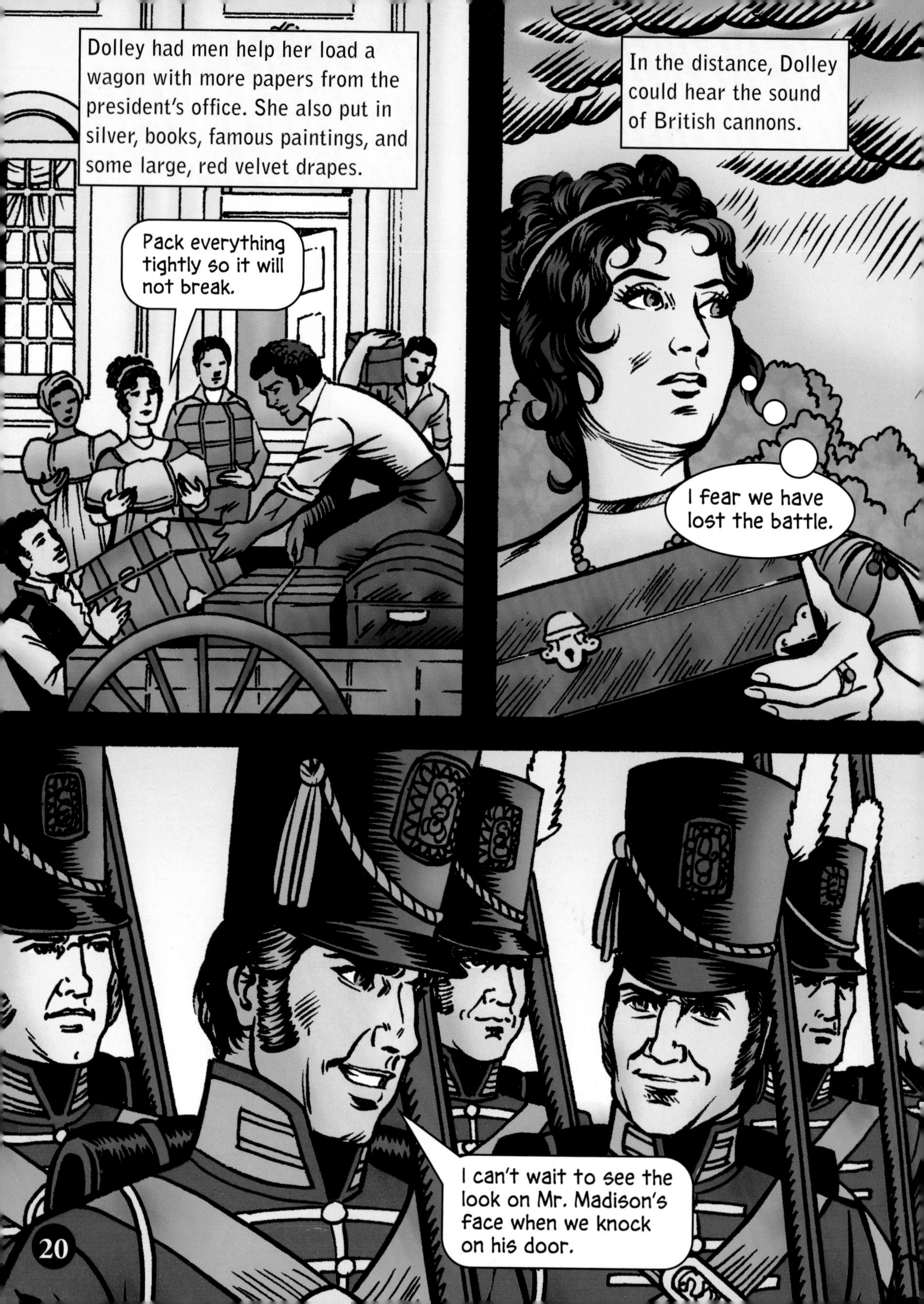
Dolley had men help her load a wagon with more papers from the president's office. She also put in silver, books, famous paintings, and some large, red velvet drapes.
Pack everything tightly so it will not break.
In the distance, Dolley could hear the sound of British cannons.
I fear we have lost the battle.
I can't wait to see the look on Mr. Madison's face when we knock on his door.

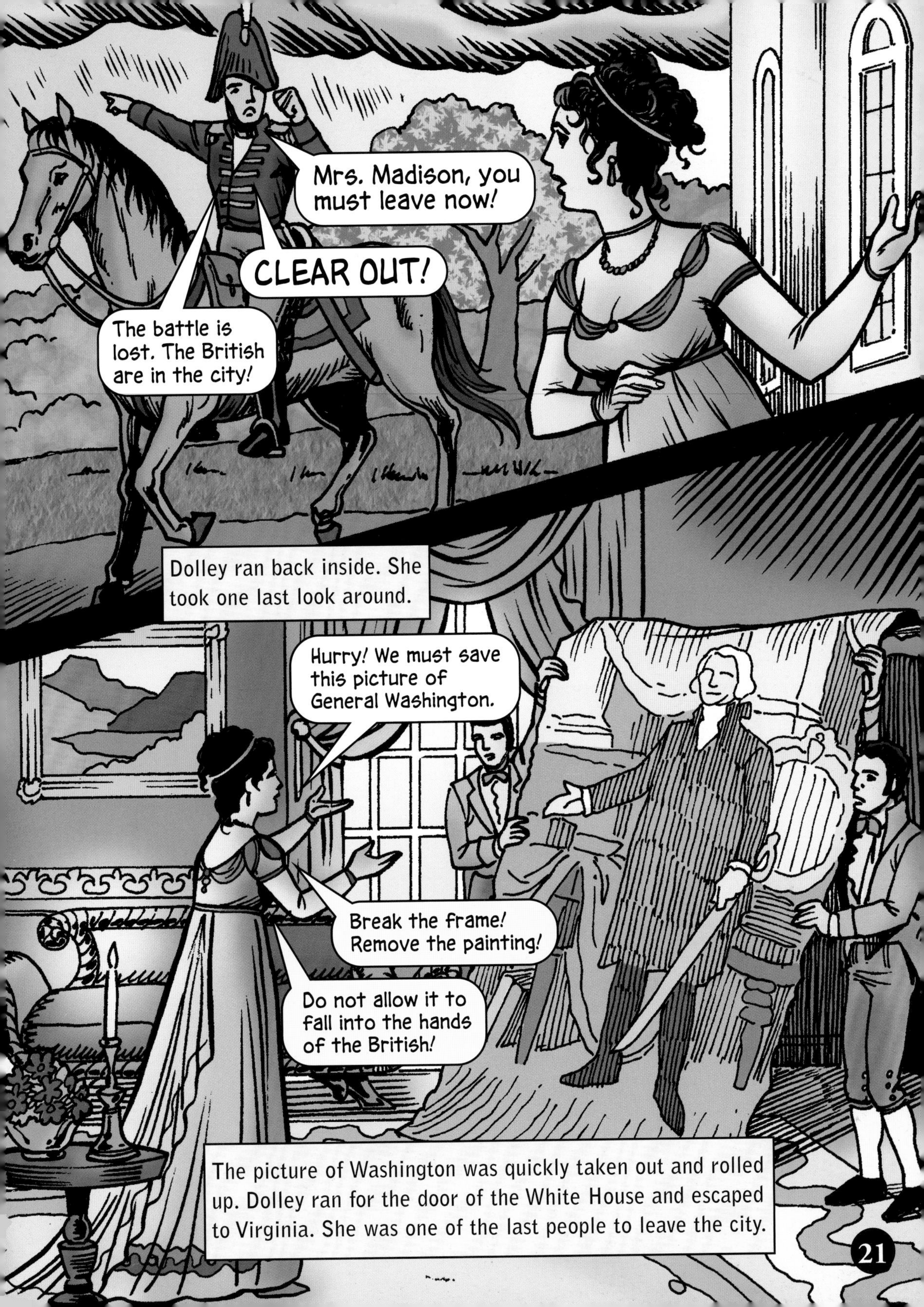

Mrs. Madison, you must leave now!
CLEAR OUT!
The battle is lost. The British are in the city!
Dolley ran back inside. She took one last look around.
Hurry! We must save this picture of General Washington.
Break the frame! Remove the painting!
Do not allow it to fall into the hands of the British!
The picture of Washington was quickly taken out and rolled up. Dolley ran for the door of the White House and escaped to Virginia. She was one of the last people to leave the city.

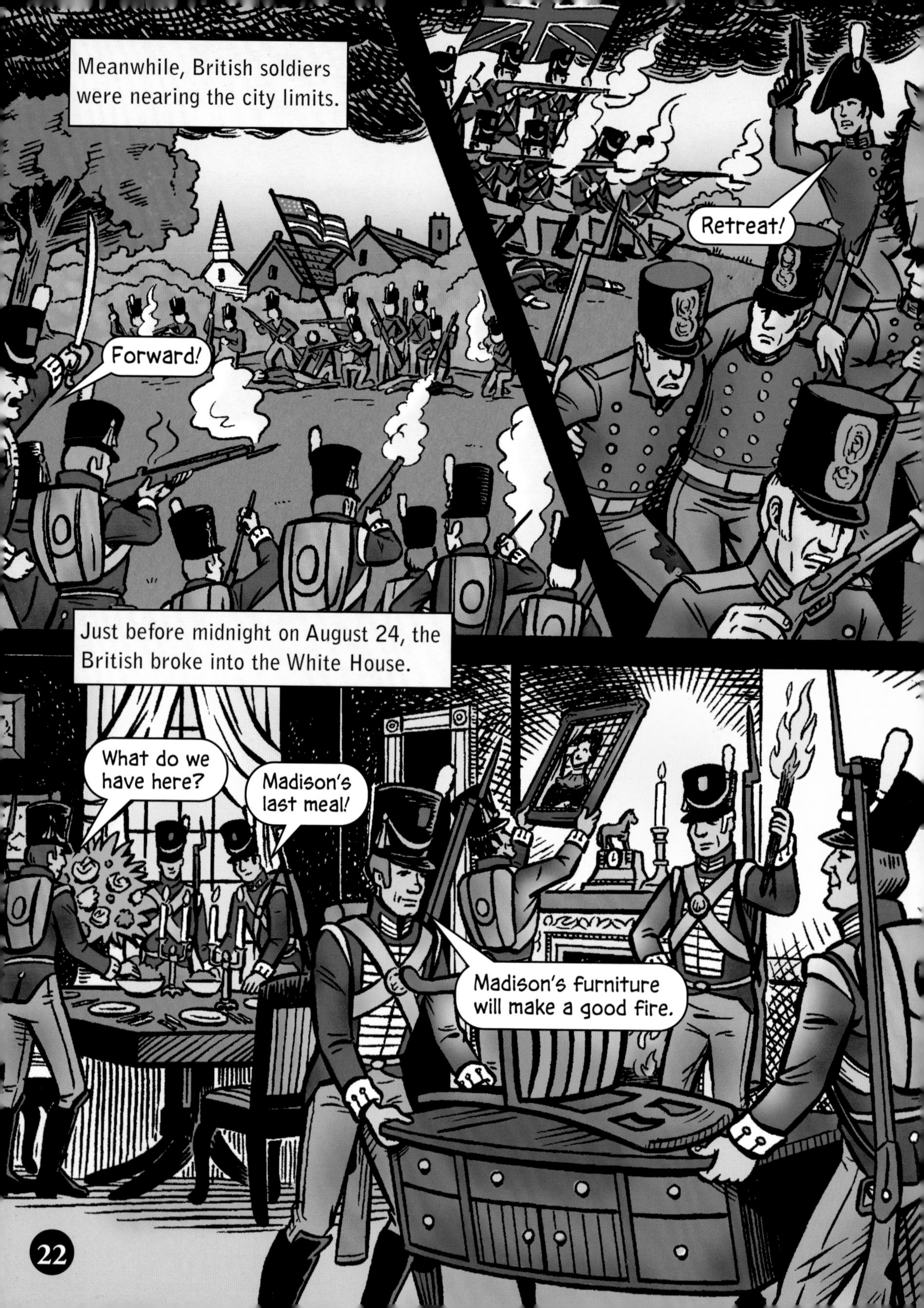
Meanwhile, British soldiers were nearing the city limits.
Forward!
Retreat!
Just before midnight on August 24, the British broke into the White House.
What do we have here?
Madison's last meal!
Madison's furniture will make a good fire.

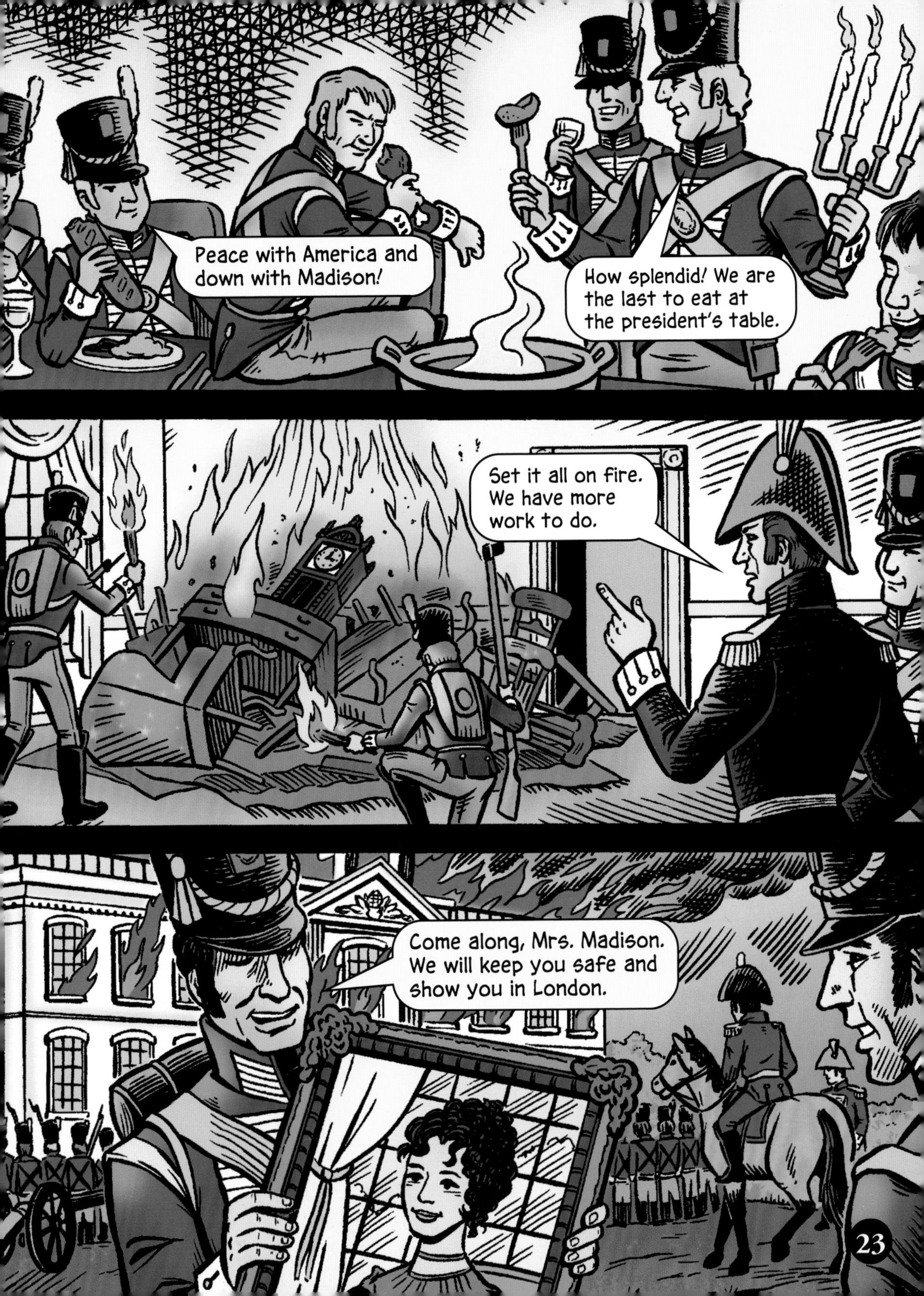
Peace with America and down with Madison!
How splendid! We are the last to eat at the president's table.
Set it all on fire. We have more work to do.
Come along, Mrs. Madison. We will keep you safe and show you in London.

Chapter 4

Dolley's Place in History

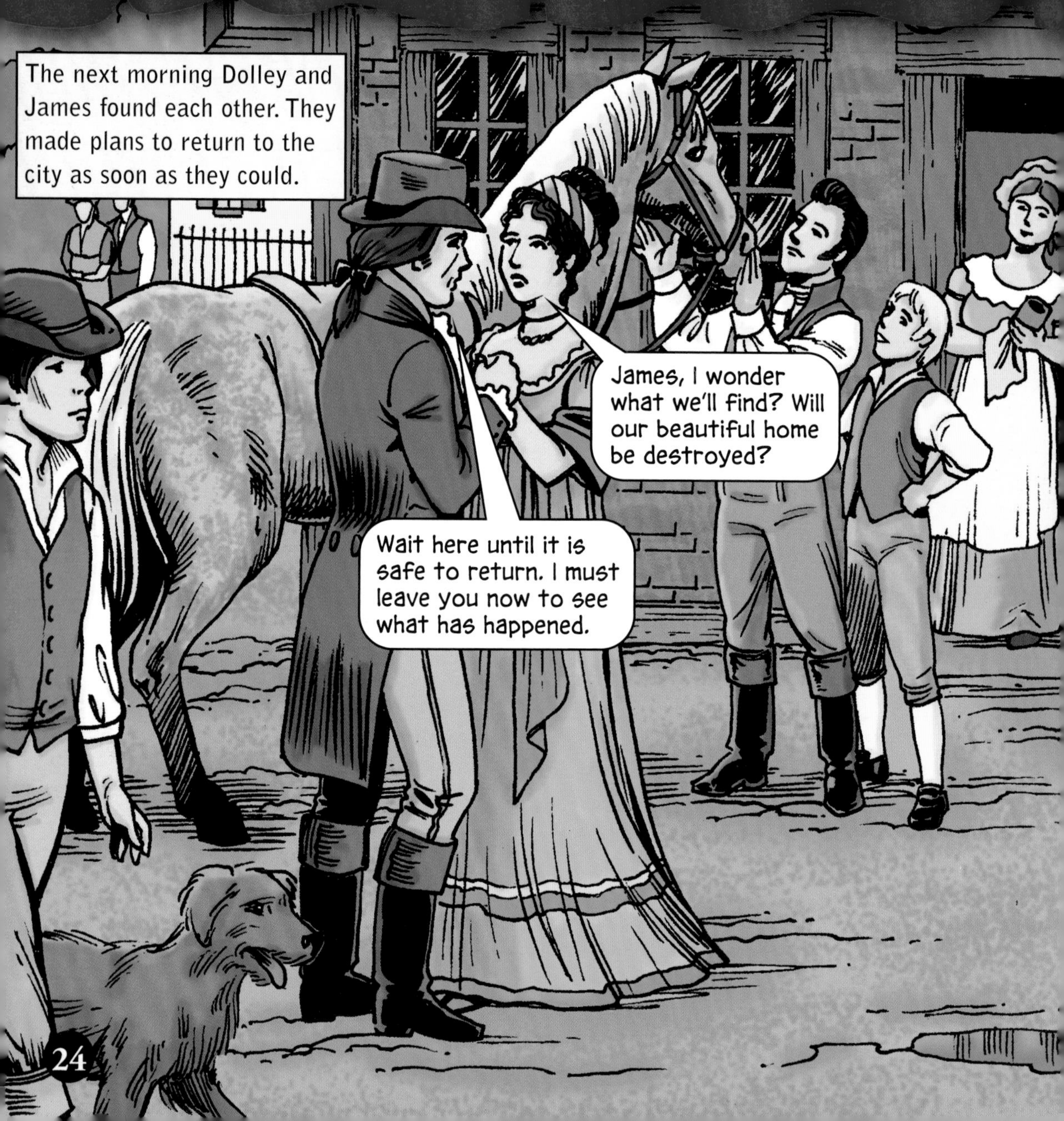
The next morning Dolley and James found each other. They made plans to return to the city as soon as they could.
James, I wonder what we'll find? Will our beautiful home be destroyed?
Wait here until it is safe to return. I must leave you now to see what has happened.

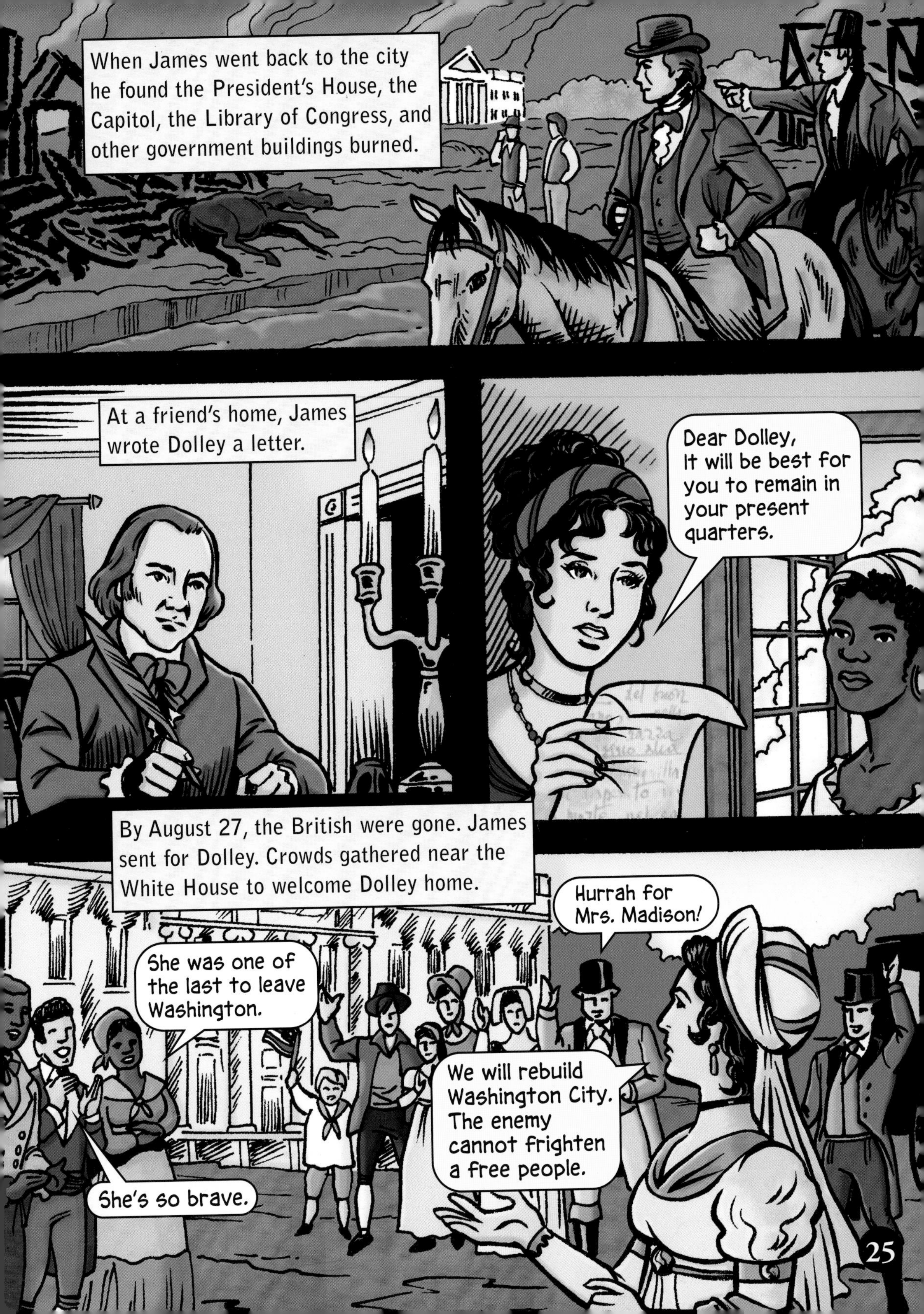

When James went back to the city he found the President's House, the Capitol, the Library of Congress, and other government buildings burned.
At a friend's home, James wrote Dolley a letter.
Dear Dolley, It will be best for you to remain in your present quarters.
By August 27, the British were gone. James sent for Dolley. Crowds gathered near the White House to welcome Dolley home.
Hurrah for Mrs. Madison!
She was one of the last to leave Washington.
We will rebuild Washington City. The enemy cannot frighten a free people.
She's so brave.

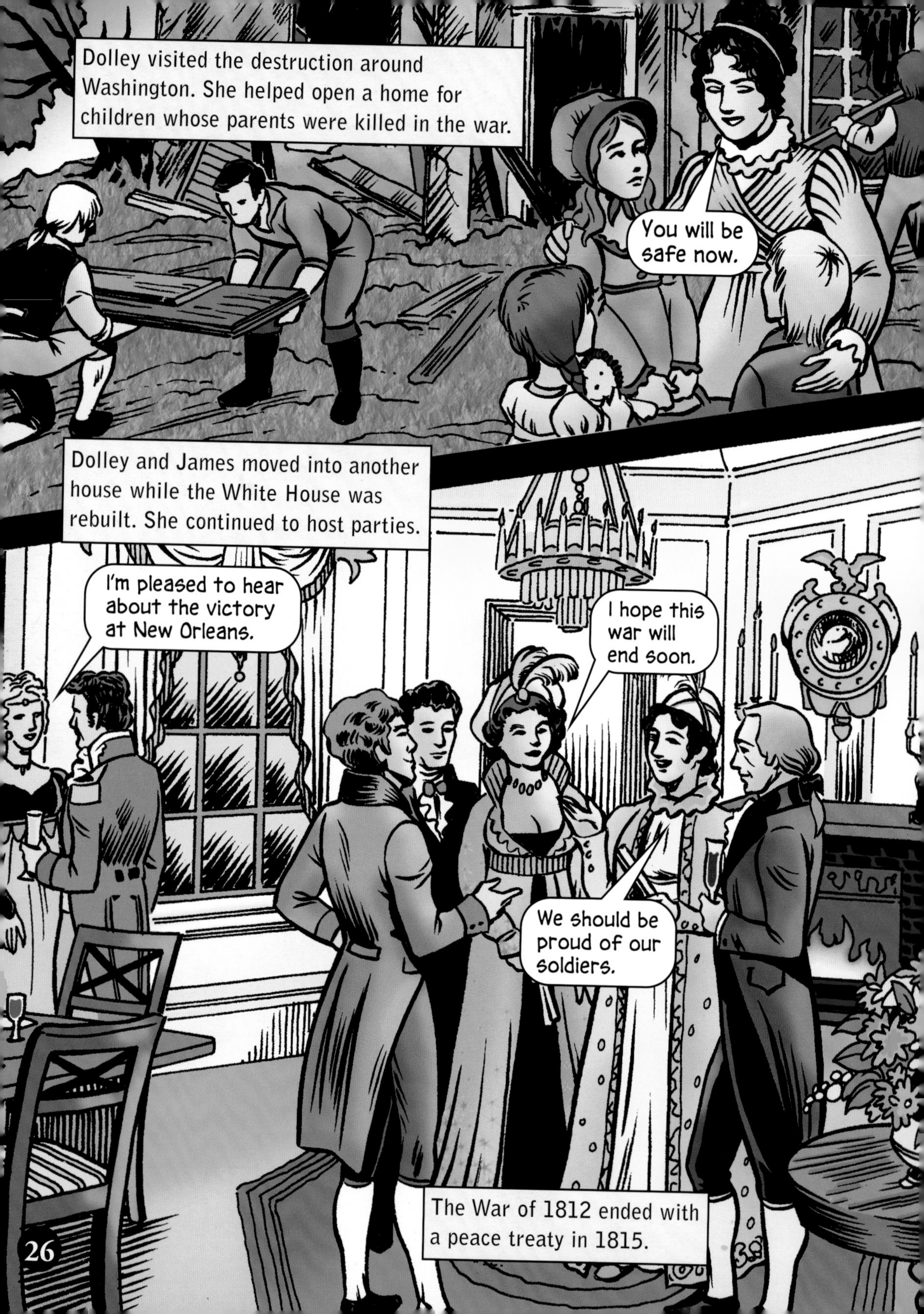
Dolley visited the destruction around Washington. She helped open a home for children whose parents were killed in the war.
You will be safe now.
Dolley and James moved into another house while the White House was rebuilt. She continued to host parties.
I'm pleased to hear about the victory at New Orleans.
I hope this war will end soon.
We should be proud of our soldiers.
The War of 1812 ended with a peace treaty in 1815.

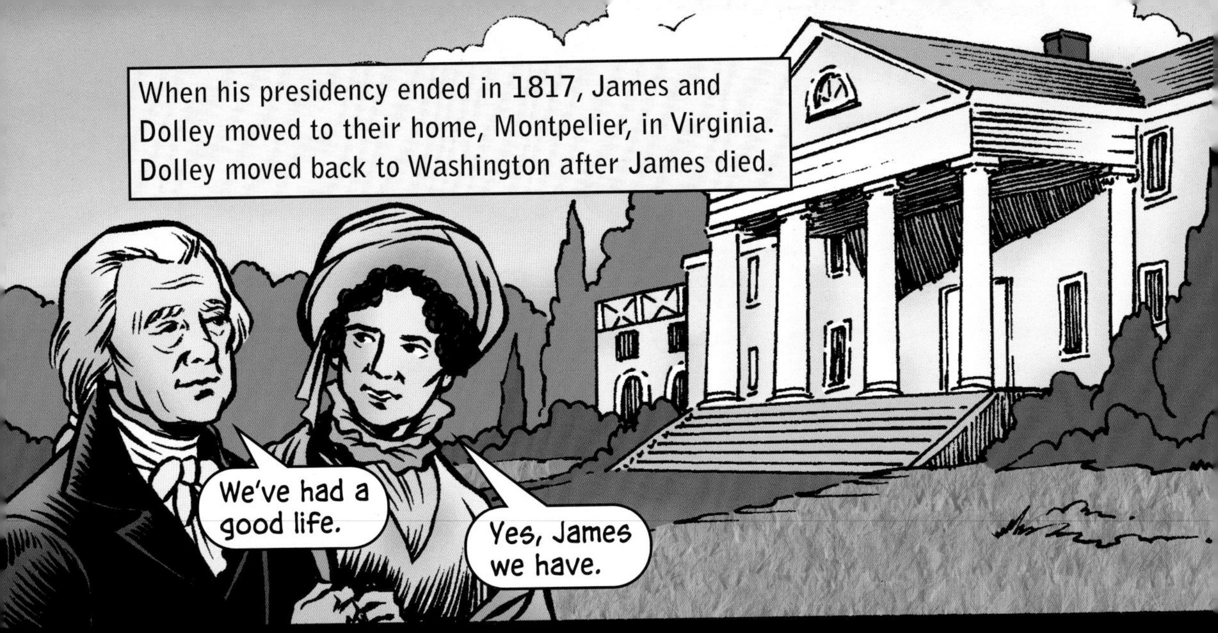
When his presidency ended in 1817, James and Dolley moved to their home, Montpelier, in Virginia. Dolley moved back to Washington after James died.
We've had a good life.
Yes, James we have.

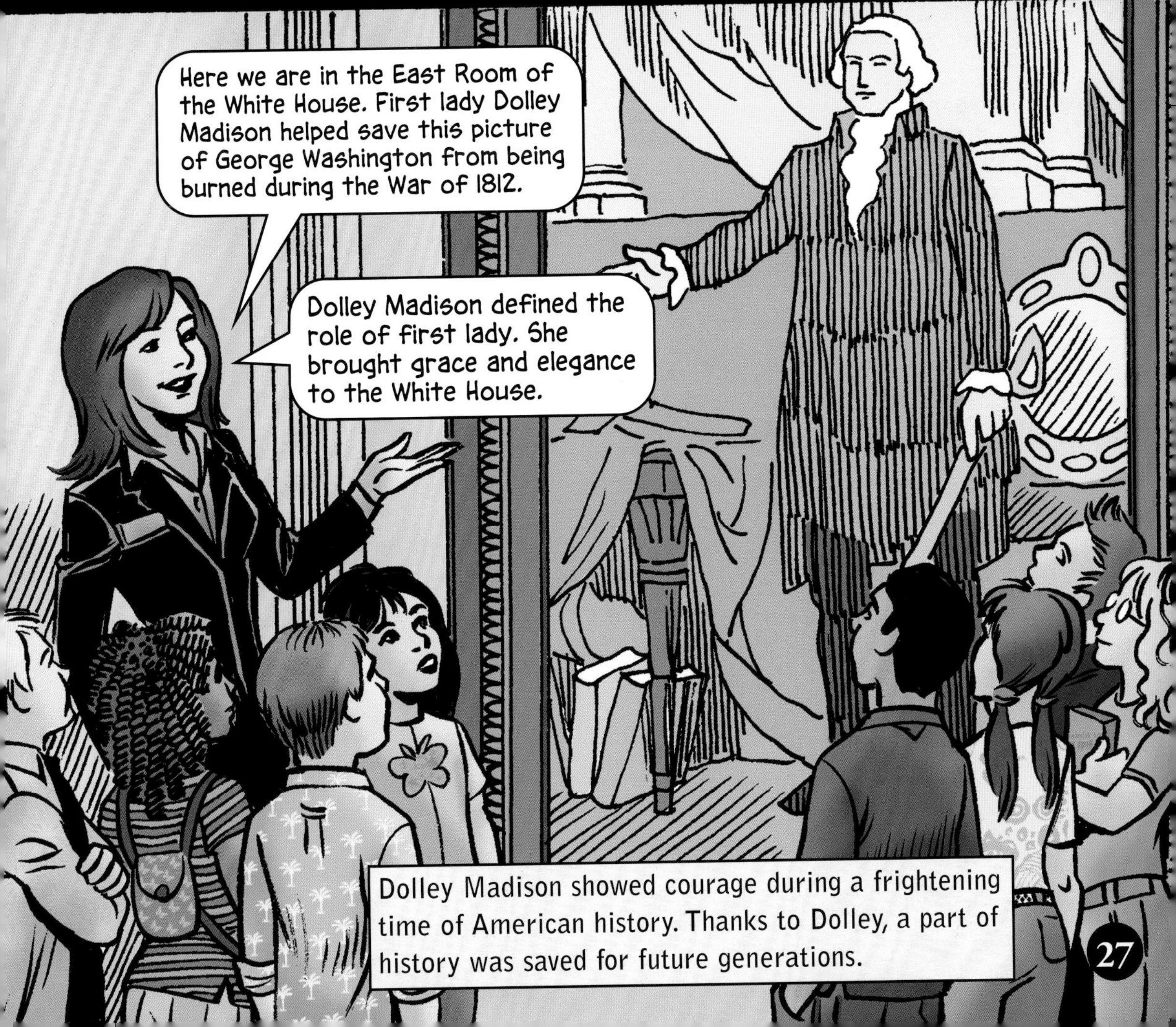
Here we are in the East Room of the White House. First lady Dolley Madison helped save this picture of George Washington from being burned during the War of 1812.
Dolley Madison defined the role of first lady. She brought grace and elegance to the White House.
Dolley Madison showed courage during a frightening time of American history. Thanks to Dolley, a part of history was saved for future generations.

More about

DOLLEY MADISON

~ Dolley was born on May 20, 1768, in North Carolina. She died on July 12, 1849. She is buried next to James at Montpelier. Today, Montpelier serves as a National Historic Site.

~ Dolley's first husband, John Todd, and son William Temple died of yellow fever. Payne Todd, Dolley's oldest son, survived.

~ Dolley hosted the first presidential inaugural ball in 1809. Tickets cost $4. More than 400 guests were invited. The Marine Band, America's oldest professional organization, played for the event. It has played for every inaugural ball since.

~ Dolley served American foods at her parties. Meals including smoked Virginia ham, baked sweet corn, Boston baked beans, and New England maple syrup were prepared. Ice cream and cake were popular desserts of the time.

- The only personal item Dolley saved from the White House before it burned was a small clock. All of her clothing and other personal belongings were left and burned.

- After the burning of the White House, James considered moving the capital back to Philadelphia. Dolley encouraged him to keep it in Washington, D.C.

- Later in her life, Dolley was given many honors for her service to the United States. On January 8, 1844, the House of Representatives gave Dolley an honorary seat in the House Chamber at the Capitol. At the time, it was the highest honor ever given to an American woman.

- Dolley was given another honor when a new invention, the telegraph, was demonstrated for the first time. She sent the first private message by telegraph.

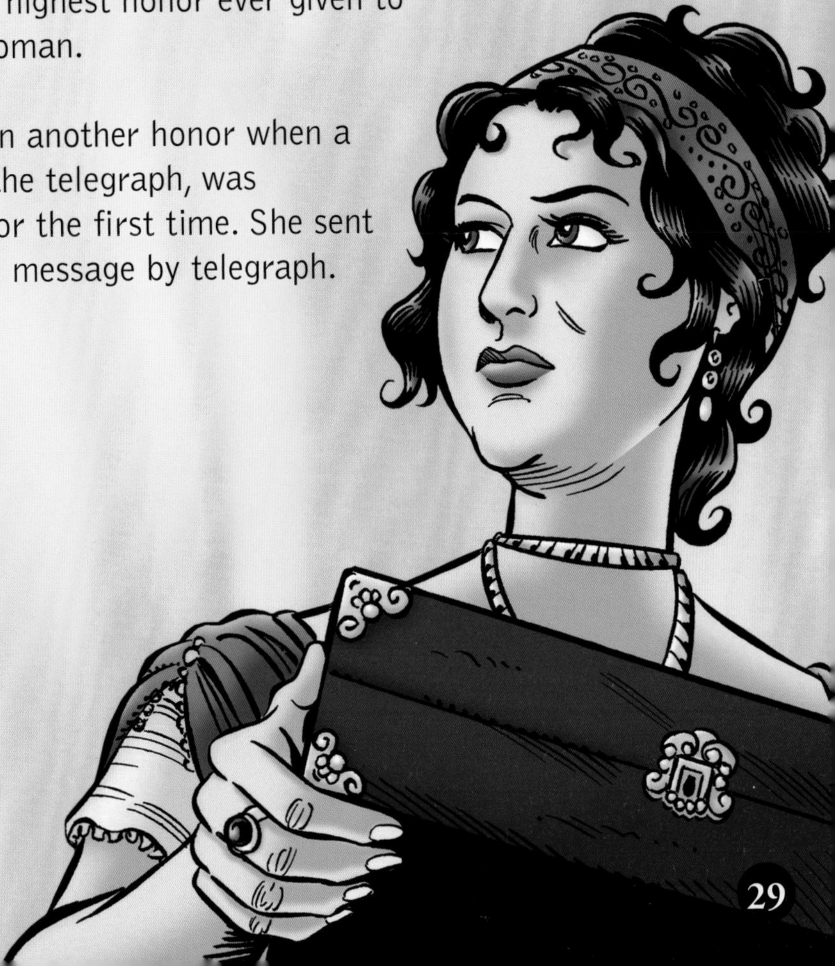

GLOSSARY

capital (KAP-uh-tuhl)—a city where the government of a country is based; Philadelphia was the capital of the United States before it was moved to Washington, D.C.

Congress (KONG-griss)—the branch of government that makes laws

fleet (FLEET)—a group of warships

hostess (HOH-stuhss)—a woman who entertains guests at parties or other social events

Quaker (KWAY-kur)—a member of the religious group also called the Society of Friends; Quakers follow simple religious services and oppose war.

INTERNET SITES

FactHound offers a safe, fun way to find Internet sites related to this book. All of the sites on FactHound have been researched by our staff.

Here's how:

1. *Visit www.facthound.com*
2. Type in this special code **0736849726** for age-appropriate sites. Or enter a search word related to this book for a more general search.
3. Click on the **Fetch It** button.

FactHound will fetch the best sites for you!

Read More

Ashby, Ruth. *James and Dolley Madison.* Presidents and First Ladies. Milwaukee: World Almanac Library, 2005.

Modifica, Lisa. *A Timeline of the White House.* Timelines of American History. New York: Rosen, 2004.

Raatma, Lucia. *The War of 1812.* We the People. Minneapolis: Compass Point Books, 2005.

Bibliography

Arnett, Ethel Stephens. *Mrs. James Madison: The Incomparable Dolley.* Greensboro, NC: Piedmont Press, 1972.

Gerson, Noel B. *The Velvet Glove: A Life of Dolley Madison.* Nashville: Thomas Nelson, 1975.

Madison, Dolley. *The Selected Letters of Dolley Payne Madison.* Charlottesville, VA: University of Virginia Press, 2003.

Pitch, Anthony S. *The Burning of Washington: The British Invasion of 1814.* Annapolis, MD: Naval Institute Press, 1998.

Smith, Margaret Bayard. *The First Forty Years of Washington Society in the Family Letters of Margaret Bayard Smith.* New York: F. Ungar, 1965.

INDEX